LAND OF THE
HORSES

LAND OF THE
HORSES

A True Story of a
Lost Soul and a
Life Found

CHRIS LOMBARD

Foreword by Joe Camp

TRAFALGAR SQUARE
North Pomfret, Vermont

First published in 2021 by
Trafalgar Square Books
North Pomfret, Vermont 05053

Disclaimer of Liability
The author and publisher shall have neither liability nor responsibility to any person or entity with respect to any loss or damage caused or alleged to be caused directly or indirectly by the information contained in this book. While the book is as accurate as the author can make it, there may be errors, omissions, and inaccuracies.

Trafalgar Square Books encourages the use of approved safety helmets in all equestrian sports and activities.

Attempts to reach the publisher of "You Just Can't See Him from the Road," select lyrics of which appear on page 147, have been made and should she be found, credit will be adjusted in subsequent editions.

Library of Congress Cataloging-in-Publication Data
Names: Lombard, Chris (Horseman), author. | Camp, Joe, writer of foreword.
Title: Land of the horses : a true story of a lost soul and a life found /
 Chris Lombard ; foreword by Joe Camp.
Description: North Pomfret, Vermont : Trafalgar Square Books, 2021. | "A prior edition was
 published by the author in 2013 under limited release." | Summary: "An intensely moving memoir
 of a young man who left heartbreak in Maine to seek healing Out West in the company of horses.
 Growing up in a small Maine town, Chris Lombard had never ridden a horse-never even touched
 one. But on one fateful night, as what he'd thought was a happy twenty-something life full of love
 and possibility fell suddenly apart, he met two horses and looked into their eyes. What he saw
 inspired him to leave everything he had, and everything he didn't have, behind, and go in search of
 what was missing. With the little he needed packed in his ten-year-old Pontiac Grand Prix, and little
 more to go on than a belief that someone would give him a chance, Chris headed west to find work
 on a horse ranch. His journey took him first to the mountains of Colorado, then the Hollywood Hills
 of California, and finally, the wild borderlands of Southern Arizona. The settings changed but the
 same lessons came in quiet moments, movingly captured in these pages: watching horses, reaching
 out to them, swinging upon their backs. Chris learned new meanings for words-presence, connection, softness, and balance-the elements of good horsemanship feeding a deep hunger he didn't
 know he had. But learning to ride a horse, learning to communicate with him, to teach him things,
 these required qualities Chris was only beginning to cultivate. Human nature plans; it pushes and it
 rushes. And it would take a terrible accident to awaken a whole new awareness for time and space,
 and Chris's place within it, beside a horse"-- Provided by publisher.
Identifiers: LCCN 2021012037 (print) | LCCN 2021012038 (ebook) | ISBN
 9781646010950 (paperback) | ISBN 9781646010967 (epub)
Subjects: LCSH: Lombard, Chris (Horseman) | Horsemen and horsewomen--West
 (U.S.)--Biography. | Horsemanship. | LCGFT: Autobiographies.
Classification: LCC SF284.52.L66 L66 2021 (print) | LCC SF284.52.L66
 (ebook) | DDC 798.2092 [B]--dc23
LC record available at https://lccn.loc.gov/2021012037
LC ebook record available at https://lccn.loc.gov/2021012038

Book design by Lauryl Eddlemon
Cover design by RM Didier
Typefaces: Myriad, Modern Sans

Printed in the United States of America

10 9 8 7 6 5 4 3 2 1

For Rocky, for all the times
I look out into the field and he is
standing there, staring at me,
and I hear the words,

You're on the right path, Chris...

————————

Contents

Foreword by Joe Camp   IX

A Time Before   1

1 | Awakened   5

2 | Innate Freedom   13

3 | Those In Our Care   19

4 | Guided   27

5 | The Fabled Demons   39

6 | Getting Closer   57

7 | Blood Paid   69

8 | Rise Again Better   81

9 | Voice of the Guardian   91

10 | Harmony   *101*

11 | Sun and Dust   *133*

12 | A Home Within   *157*

13 | The Deepest Gladness   *183*

Acknowledgments   *193*

About the Author   *195*

Foreword

WHEN YOU DISCOVER someone who cares as much about the horse and who knows as much about the horse as Chris Lombard, you cannot help but wonder how it all came about. What brought him to this perfect point of truly understanding the relationship with the horse and fully knowing how to lead humans to that point, each in their own special way?

I suppose I wondered all this aloud one too many times because Chris asked if I would like to read this book, and perhaps consider writing its foreword.

I was honored. But I really didn't want to do it. I wanted no part of it, actually. I'm a very harsh critic, first and foremost of myself. I am brutal with myself about my writing and often hate myself for treating myself so poorly. But I'm also brutal with what I read by others. If I pick up a book that doesn't reach out and grab me by the throat and pull me immediately, without choice, into a new and emotional adventure, that book usually gets dropped on the floor, and I reach for another one in the stack. I want to care about what I read and who I read about. I want them to take me on a journey that I cannot resist and cannot wait to get back to. I want them to fill my senses—and cause me to reach for a better me.

How could any of that happen here?

This was Chris Lombard's first book.

I spent years and years learning to write, for movies and television, studying what makes a good story and experimenting with emotion and how to reach it. All before I ever attempted my first book.

What Chris was asking me to do would surely result in the loss of a friendship.

And there's no way I could lie.

How could this young whippersnapper burp out a first book that I could actually praise in a foreword?

You are about to find out.

Because do it he did.

And you will be so much better off for having experienced it.

This book changed my life.

And it will change yours.

Joe Camp

Author of the National Bestseller
The Soul of a Horse: Life Lessons from the Herd
and creator of the canine superstar Benji and
writer-director-producer of all five Benji movies

Alto's eyes scanned the hills. He too knew they were close.
His chestnut coat and white blaze had turned fuzzy with the cold
weather. The tall and lanky, tough desert ranch horse...I softly laid my
hand on his neck and his left eye looked back to me and
there it was—that feeling I would get with a horse.

Something all the way right.

THE DIRT ROAD TO THE FARMHOUSE was dark and tangled. I turned on the dome light to look at the directions she had given me. The windows were down, letting in a cool breeze and the sound of car wheels over gravel. Like a flashlight in a cave the headlights lit the road and the walls of thick Maine woods to each side, and I watched the farm appear out of the darkness. I hoped the drive would be longer, just a bit more road. I wanted time. Maybe to think about what I wanted to say. Maybe to just delay the inevitable.

As I walked up to the front door, I felt like I was going into the job interview of a lifetime.

"Did you find the place okay?" Allison asked as I stepped inside.

"Yes," I said. I was nervous, that twist in my stomach like when we were on our first date. Her hair was down over her shoulders. Long, dark, with that slight curl at the bottom it sometimes had. Usually in the mornings. Perfectly spread over the pillow beside me.

She was house-sitting, taking care of the farm and its animals. She asked if I would like something to drink and then silently showed me around, going through the motions as if we were mere acquaintances. Neither one of us made the move to talk, letting the thickness in the air grow. And then, like she didn't know what else to do, she said it was time to take care of the horses…I could come with her to the barn if I wanted.

Allison fed the two horses while I sneezed and rubbed my itchy, watering eyes. Hay fever. It hit the moment I even thought about going near a barn.

"Wow. Horses are big," I said, nose all stuffed up.

"They are but they don't know it," she replied as she filled their water buckets.

I stood there, eyes feeling puffy and red. The horses were beautiful in their form; I couldn't believe this was the first time in my life I had seen one up close. I suddenly felt foolish for not ever doing this before. I liked their sounds and motions while they ate. It made me feel good. They would grab a bite of hay and then raise their heads to look at me while they chewed, then grab another bite and raise their heads again to look at me, all very content in… their world.

"I'm going back to the house," Allison said. *We need to get on with this* was in her eyes.

I turned to follow but as I was closing the barn door I looked back. The horses were still chewing while they watched me leave, and there was something in their eyes. It wasn't like a human. But it wasn't like an animal either.

Back in the house Allison and I finally sat down across from each other. As I looked at her not wanting to look at me, little memories came back. Her giggling while she ran and slid across my wood floor in her cozy wool socks. That content little smile she had whenever she was shopping for vegetables. The innocent look on her face when she was watching a movie she was really into.

"You're not ready to be in a committed relationship," she said. "You're searching for something else."

"No, Ally, I know what I want in life and—"

"I don't think you do. There's something in you that…" She paused but didn't look up. "I love you but there's something in you that isn't all the way here."

Her eyes stared at the floor as if studying the wood. Then, like she had come to some end thought, she said, "I can't do this anymore," and stood up, walking toward the doorway where she turned and finally looked into my eyes. We stayed like that for a long moment.

"This is the end," she said.

Lying in bed that night, I gazed blankly at the ceiling. *Did that really just happen? Why did I mess it all up? What was wrong with me?* I couldn't move, couldn't blink, my heart was catatonic.

Suddenly I thought about those horses out in the barn, and I knew what it was I had seen in their eyes. Contentment. They didn't want to be anything more than they were. And this contentment wasn't something they had found or been given.

They were born with it.

1 | Awakened

I NEVER KNEW how fragile it all was.

I had always thought I was a confident, happy guy. I had lots of friends, a great job, made good money. But in the months after the breakup so much was exposed in me. So little strength. So many fears. Not enough hope. Something was missing and I started to think it had been missing for a long time.

I drank a lot. I ate mostly fast food or pizza. And I seemed to lose the ability to dispose of the empty pizza boxes. They just ended up scattered across the floor. Many nights I found myself lying among them. I didn't shower much. I grew a beard. I didn't decide to grow a beard—it just happened. It was the inevitable sidekick to not showering much. And then the bar I worked at closed down, leaving me jobless, which meant I had a whole lot more time to lie among empty pizza boxes and work on my beard.

Through it all I just couldn't get those two horses out of my head. I would be lying on the floor staring at the ceiling and suddenly I would be thinking about the sounds and the smells and the feeling I got in the barn the night Ally and I broke up. The way the horses were staring at me with those eyes. Like they knew me better than I did.

The days turned cold and winter came and I was numb. I walked in the woods a lot. Alone was where I wanted to be, and the forest had always been the only place I could be alone but not feel alone. I desperately wanted to be moved by the beauty and invigoration of nature, but the hills, the trees, the rivers... they did not make me feel good anymore. The sunrises and sunsets were empty.

One day, with no place else to go, I ended up at my father's grave. He'd died of brain cancer when I was thirteen. I thought about the funeral, so packed it was standing room only and some people had to wait outside. He was a state police officer, a well-known man, a respected man with many friends. I remembered walking out of the church and seeing all the state troopers standing in formation and how they, and all the others in attendance, followed my mom and me as we walked through town to the cemetery. It felt so long ago—a different life. I tried hard to remember the sound of my father's voice but couldn't. The thing I remembered easily was that he was a good man.

I stood at his grave, frustrated. *What had I made of my life?*

Suddenly, I could see him there. I could see him looking me straight in the eye.

His gaze was strong with unflinching belief. All he had lived for. All he had believed in. He was gone, but everything he lived for and believed in… was not.

Enough, I could hear him saying, now remembering his voice—its pace and pitch. *What happens to you in life does not define you. The choices you make and the actions you take do.*

It finally made sense. What I was going through had nothing to do with Allison or the breakup.

It had to do with me.

And it was time to make a choice.

I sneezed twice. My nose was running, and my eyes were itching like crazy.

"Are you allergic?" asked Anna, the riding instructor.

"Hay fever," I replied, like it didn't matter.

Behind Anna was a rather large horse. His name was Oberon. He was a bay Thoroughbred gelding, and he was about to be the first horse I had ever ridden. Anna took me through the grooming routine and showed me how to saddle him. Then we walked out to the riding arena.

As I gathered the reins in my left hand and placed my foot in the stirrup, I paused for a moment and looked into Oberon's eye. Just like the two horses in the barn, it had a locking effect on me, drawing me in.

I breathed in and stepped up and swung my leg over his back. And as I sat in the saddle I breathed out, and something clicked into place.

I rode Oberon as he walked in a circle, and from what Anna was saying, I was doing well, except for the twenty times she reminded me to look up and breathe. At moments I was entirely lost in what I was feeling. The gentleness in how the big bay carried me. The softness in how little this thousand-pound animal needed to guide him. The simple grace in the rhythmic sway of his back as he walked. The perfection of it.

How is this possible, I thought, *this horse allowing me to sit on him and tell him what to do when I have no idea what I am doing? What is this? What is going on here?*

"Okay," Anna said. "That's good for today. Great job."

Oberon came to a halt, and I went to dismount, but as soon as my feet touched the ground, it hit me. It all came back. The hurt and the pain.

But while I was on Oberon... it hadn't been there.

"When can I come back?" I quickly asked.

I went home that day and made myself a salad. I picked up the empty pizza boxes off the floor. Took a shower and shaved. And then I grabbed the car keys and drove out to my mom's house.

"Colorado?" she said like it was on the moon.

"Yeah. Bart has a house there and he asked me to come out a while back."

"And what are you going to do in Colorado?"

I paused for a second, thinking about how it would sound. "I'm going to look for work on a horse ranch."

"What? You don't have any experience with... *anything* on a horse ranch."

"I work hard. I'm honest and reliable. Somebody will give me a chance."

My mother shook her head. She had seen me go through many phases. Breakdancing. Skateboarding. Bartending. A career in criminal justice. And now it sounded like I wanted to join the rodeo.

"Mom, something is... going on here. I don't know what it is, but something is opening up here for me, and this is my chance. I have to go to Colorado, I know it. I don't know what will happen, I don't. But I know it will be good."

She looked at me intently and I felt a test of my resolve. She had always been there for me, supporting me in everything I wanted to do. She might not have understood me right then, but she believed in me.

"Do you think the car will make a trip like that," she asked with a skeptical eye.

"The Grand Prix? It's only ten years old with two hundred thousand miles on it... and has gotten me everywhere I've ever needed to be," I replied with a grin.

She smiled back. "A horse ranch, huh? What in the world ever brought you to that?"

I looked at her very matter-of-factly.

"Horses," I said.

It was afternoon and the highway had been straight for a while. On either side were rolling hills covered with thick, tall grass swaying in the wind. Bluest blue sky stretching forever. The few clouds only made it more perfect.

I was in the West. The Black Hills of South Dakota.

Dusk started to set in. The land darkened but the sky was still powder blue with the daylight struggling to stay alive. The cars around me were all cruising at the same speed, in formation like a flock of birds drawn west. Most with headlights on now. The highway rose to take us over a hill, and when we got to the top, there was a sunset like I had never seen. The sun had just gone down, its last gasp casting a sharp glow of red to the bellies of the clouds that hovered over the horizon.

The sky was on fire. Soaking it up like blood into sand.

The cars around me slowed, and I knew everybody was seeing this just as I was. Within that moment we were suddenly bound, a kinship of travelers, side by side. The sunset by itself was not complete. It needed the highway pointed toward it, carrying all of us, to make it whole. When the car in front of me pulled off at the next exit, I felt something weaken.

That night I camped and sat by the fire as it crackled and glowing embers floated into the dark and faded away. I stared into the flames, got up and worked the fire, and then sat back down, crossing my arms and staring some more. *You're searching for something else,* Allison had said. *You're not all the way here.*

In the morning I was packing to leave the campground when I noticed a stable of horses a ways off and a cowboy saddling some of them. To his side stood two touristy-looking folks. I wandered over, asked what was going on, and the cowboy said they did trail rides. I asked if I could come along.

"Would love to have ya," he replied.

My horse was a tall sorrel Quarter Horse named Charlie. The cowboy's name was Seth. He wore a black Stetson that kept his eyes hidden. He looked to be around forty, but it was hard to tell if the lines on his face were from years or from living. The trail was mostly wooded, rocky at points, with ups and downs to keep us awake. Seth was quiet much of the time, but every now and then he would talk of the history of the hills.

At the end of the ride the two other people went on their way, and I was about to myself when Seth quietly spoke in my direction. "You wanna help with the horses?"

"Sure!" I answered, too excitedly.

He passed me the reins to one of the horses and then started unsaddling the other three. I followed suit, watching to see how he did it. We then walked the horses to a water trough.

All was quiet as they sipped. Just the sound of the horses drinking. A slow, rhythmic gurgle. A pause now and then as one lifted his head to look around, a trickle of water dripping from damp lips back to the water. Seth and I stood in silence, but I sensed a difference in our silences. I was uncomfortable. I was scraping around in my head for anything to say, some topic of conversation. Seth, though, didn't appear to have any problem with the silence. He seemed to prefer it.

I sneezed twice. My nose stuffed up, my eyes itchy.

"You allergic?" he asked.

"Hay fever," I replied, like it didn't matter.

I spent the next night in Montana, and then crossed the Beartooth Pass into Cooke City, moving on to Yellowstone. I went on another trail ride. This time there were thirty of us in one long line with four "wranglers," as they were called. We waded through open grasslands and rode high into rising hills lined with tall pines and spruce.

After the ride the horses were tied to a long rail, and they stood there, quiet in their own world. I stood outside the fence and looked at them. Then I looked at the people milling around me. I sensed a separation between them—the tourists walking away, the wranglers laughing and talking about the next trip, and the horses waiting quietly.

The people were not aware of the horses' world.
The horses were very much aware of theirs.

That's where we all begin, staring at the horse from outside the fence.

We know horses live by a nature that is pure and honest. That they are individuals with feelings. That they value their lives as much as we do ours. That they have inherent fears. And we know they connect to other living things, including humans.

To understand them is to understand ourselves. Understanding that connection will get us where we want to be. In learning how to guide the horse, we will make mistakes and get frustrated, mad at ourselves, mad at the horse, and feel lost… and this is all natural. We will need help, and that's okay. It will be there, in some form, when we ask.

A lot of times there is a difference in us from outside to inside. But horses will not hide anything, and they won't let us hide anything either. With a horse we are who we are. The horse shows us our strengths and draws out our weaknesses—and if we open up to the horse, he will help us overcome those weaknesses. We must welcome and be accepting of that.

So much is done from outside the fence. The work of how we treat life and everything and everybody in it. The work of knowing who we are and what our intentions are. Something happens there, looking at the horse from outside the fence. The most inspiring of moments.

A beginning.

2 | Innate Freedom

THE FIRST STEP in asking horses to stay with us? Giving them the freedom to leave.

Individuality, a love of life, strong spirit. Horses are our equals in these. To think ourselves above them is to limit all life has to offer us. To hold them as equals is to open every door.

And it starts with you and the horse together, free.

Just hang out. Meet each other. Interact. See what happens. Get to know each other on equal ground. Ask nothing of him. You could be in the pasture, in the riding arena, or in the round pen. Any enclosure will do. You may have a carrot with you. You may try and find where the horse loves to be scratched. You may give him some hay or take him to a paddock where there is grass. Watching the horse is learning about the horse. Starting your interaction with the horse like this will show his whole self to you, inside and out. And in this interaction the horse will also see the *real* you.

We have to first see in ourselves what we wish to see in our horses. So if we are hoping to someday have the horse respect us and our wishes, then it begins with us respecting ourselves. If we live by actions of kindness, honesty, and patience, then we carry ourselves with a certain presence. We are more relaxed, more composed, more steady, and we have self-respect. Our relationship with horses begins with how we choose to live every moment of our lives.

A lot of people have become desensitized to what horses do for us. They have grown to just expect obedience. They have lost the ability to notice the vacant and detached look in a horse's eyes from years of learned helplessness. Those eyes should be free, empowered, alive, and wanting more. They should *look* for the human.

It takes time to get to where we have a relationship with a horse that he enjoys as much as anything else in his life. Where if he were given the choice he would still choose to be with us. In first meetings, if he is free and we give him the choice, many times he will walk away. Doubt will creep into us. *What if he is right? What if I have nothing special to offer him? What if I don't know what I'm doing? What if he is better off without me?*

When I am with a horse, I believe in what I have to offer. And when I go into a pen or paddock with a horse, I believe that someday he will believe in me and trust me. A minute, a day, a week, a month, a year…we must let go of time and get to just *feeling* for the beginning of connection. We need a certain level of understanding of horsemanship to be safe around the horse, but our connection with him begins with where we're coming from on the inside.

How long will it take a horse to trust us? The answer is up to him.

How much patience should we have during this process? There is only one true answer. It's an answer we feel more than know.

And once we feel it, the horse will too.

In the middle of the night I drove into Highlands Ranch, Colorado. I pulled into my friend Bart's driveway, got out of the Grand Prix, and stood resting my hand on the hood. I was in a new land and I felt free. Bart emerged from the front door with a smile. He was a man who made it a big part of his life to be there when needed. And he *knew* me. A simple thing to say, rare to find.

Some of the closest people to you, they still do not truly know you. They have to ask questions. They wonder. They assume. But they do not *know*.

Bart knew.

"Great to see you, man," he said. "I'm happy you're here. Leave your stuff in the car for now and come on in and tell me about these last days on the road."

We sat out back on his patio. It was early July and the stars in Colorado's front range sky were beaming. There was a touch of a light breeze, the air of something settling.

"So what's the plan, man?" asked Bart. "Are you really going to try and find work on a horse ranch?"

"Yeah, I figured I would see if I could make it happen for a while here, then maybe head to California and give those screenplays I've written a shot."

"Gotta say, it's really awesome what you're doing, going in all the way with what's inspiring you. You discover horses and then you drive to Colorado."

Bart was not one to spend time on the thin surface-level of things, conversation included. He wasn't just giving me a place to stay. He was invested in my journey.

The next day I got to work finding the job I envisioned. I was ready to shovel manure, stack hay, and fill water buckets, so I opened my computer and like a telemarketer called every horse ranch listed within forty miles.

"I'm a hard worker, I learn quickly, and you won't find anybody that is more honest and reliable and—"

When they heard I had no experience, they weren't interested. Apparently, there were a lot of other people in Colorado who could work on ranches who had actually ridden horses for longer than three months.

After a couple of weeks of trying, I just plain needed a job. I saw an ad for a children's program director at an elementary school. They needed somebody to run their before-and-after-school-care program for kids, eight to twelve years old. The hours were six-thirty to nine in the morning and four to six-thirty in the afternoon. I had no experience with this sort of work, either, but I had always thought I was good with children. And hanging out with some kids for a few hours in the morning and the afternoon...how hard could it be? It seemed the hiring committee felt I could get by on my enthusiasm. The job was mine.

It was a Monday morning when I began my first day running the program. Parents arrived with their kids at the school cafeteria, the program's base of operations. Some wanted to chat, most just dropped their children off and ran. Some kids had homework they had to finish, others played games. It seemed they knew the routine. Soon enough the bell rang for school to begin, and the twelve kids jumped up and filed out of the room without even saying goodbye. Job done.

This was going to be easy, just like I thought.

That afternoon was the same. Kids trotted into the room and had a snack then went to play games, do homework, or otherwise busy themselves with friends and activities. It was a little loud but nothing too crazy. They still hadn't really noticed me so I decided to try and talk to them, moving around the room from group to group to check in. The children seemed only half-heartedly interested in me, though. I had been told the program had seen a lot of people come and go, so for all they knew, I would be gone tomorrow. But I wanted them to feel free with me, that they could approach and talk to me about anything.

Parents began to arrive, and the kids once again just grabbed their bags and left without saying goodbye. It felt...hollow. Like I was just a watchman, a guard, just a set of eyes to make sure they didn't run off.

Was it really supposed to be like this?

"Sounds to me they're just used to the program director not caring," said Bart. "Have you ever worked with kids before?"

"Not really," I said. "But I've always gotten along with them well enough."

"If you're paying attention to them while letting them get to know you, they'll open up sooner or later. It just takes time. They gotta see it for more than a few days. Patience combined with consistency, you know?"

With half an hour left before school the next morning, a few kids said they wanted to go to the gym to play a game of kickball. I was all for it, hoping it would help get them to like me.

The game was going great. Then an argument broke out. I attempted to politely intervene. The arguers ignored me and got louder. The kids began going their separate ways. I attempted to pull kickball back together, but no one listened.

It got louder.

Some kids started to climb the ropes tied along one wall of the gym, and some kids wandered toward the door to the cafeteria. I asked them to stop climbing. I asked them not to leave. They must not have heard me.

Then someone was crying. Suddenly a ball went sailing through the air and conked a girl in the head. Now she was crying too. Several boys began running around, throwing the ball at the girls, who screamed and ran away. As I chased after the boys I glanced toward one corner of the gym and saw a bunch of children all jumbled up in a pile. I paused for a second, standing in the middle of the chaos, realizing I had somehow discovered the power of invisibility.

"Hey! What's going on in here!" came a thunderous voice.

Mr. Ray was the school maintenance man. He was also the school sheriff. He was tall and lanky, with gray hair and a full gray beard, and he wore a very tight sweater. He had piercing eyes that burned you with their judgment and contempt. And he was now standing in the doorway to the gym.

The kids all stopped what they were doing and froze, eyes wide. It was as if an angry lion had entered the room.

"What's going on in here?" he demanded again.

Nobody answered. Nobody moved. A ball slowly bounced and settled on the floor. Then I realized I was the one who had to answer. Me, standing amongst the kids, just as frozen, just as scared.

"Uh, I'm the new director of the…um…the before- and after-school program, and I'm…we're playing kickball, and it's just…we, um…I…" I stopped trying to talk and just smiled like you do when you know you are about to get in trouble.

Mr. Ray didn't smile back. His tight sweater looked like it was going to burst off him at any moment like the Incredible Hulk's t-shirt.

"You keep things under control in here!" he said sternly, looking me in the eye. "Or *I* will." He then slowly turned and walked out.

Mr. Ray was all about leadership by action. And it worked. The kids went easy from there on out that morning.

The afternoon found me back at the school. The bell rang and the kids came trotting into the room, but whereas the morning session started off quiet and ended crazy, the afternoon session started crazy right off.

First came snack time (feeding frenzy), then a bit of homework (yeah, right) and then into the gym for playing and games (mayhem). My objective soon became damage control as they ran around, ran into each other, fell down, and cried. I mumbled directions now and then but no one listened. They didn't even look at me. They didn't take my words as orders—not even as advice.

I was two days in and it had gotten out of control. Fast.

As the parents arrived for pick-up, I wondered what they thought. I carefully studied their eyes for disdain or dismay while behind me one kid painted on the wall and another danced on a table. To my surprise, the parents didn't seem to think anything of it.

Was it always like this?

After the last kid left, I sat down on the floor, completely spent. There was a shoe print on my jeans. I had literally been run over.

"This is not for me," I said, defeated.

3 | Those In Our Care

WE HAVE COME TO UNDERSTAND that our power is not found in changing the world to accommodate us. The power to create change is found elsewhere. It's found in that simplest yet most challenging of places.

Inside ourselves.

The most respect we can give horses is in how we care for them. Many times, when horses are frustrated, challenged, or dangerous, it can be traced back to them being unhealthy, unhappy, or neglected. Horses are domesticated, yes, but they evolved as wild animals. A species that spent fifty-five million years living in herds, moving constantly over wide open land in a certain type of climate while eating naturally growing forage without any humans around. Basically, domestication, even when born into it, can be a big challenge for a horse.

We all do the best we can with what we know and have, but the care comes down to knowing an individual horse as best we can and understanding what he needs to be happy and healthy. From there, we should then model his care as closely as we can to how he would naturally live in the wild. Domestication can provide a lot of benefits and assistance for a horse—steady meals and a roof go a long way—but horses survived amazingly well for a very long time without our help. Not eating just two meals. Not eating sugar-filled grain. Not wearing metal shoes nailed to their feet so they carry us better. Not wearing ill-fitted saddles. Not foundering or colicking. Not cribbing. Not anxiety-ridden with ulcers lining their stomachs.

There are certain key elements for horse health—herd interaction, movement, and grazing. If they have buddies of some sort, if they are engaged and moving and making choices, and if they have steady access to forage for most of their day, then they seem to maintain an inner balance. Stalls, corrals, separation, grain, and shoes should all be used only when it is to benefit a specific horse's health. Some horses are given second life with therapeutic shoes, and some horses love the protection their stalls provide. But the tools of domestication should not be indiscriminately applied to horses simply for the human's convenience or just because they can be.

We need to respect our horses as the individuals they are. Some horses are scared and some are confident. Some don't like to be scratched on the face, others do. Some horses are built for dressage and some just like to play games and do tricks. Some believe in you right off, some need time. They may all be bound by the same nature, but they are all different in personality, physicality, and experience.

If we truly love our horses, their care is more important than what they can do for us. And caring for a horse takes a lot of time and money, and inevitably involves some blood, sweat, and even tears. Sometimes a lot of tears. But it's worth it. And when the adventures come you will walk the road together, not just horse and human, but as two friends who are in it for each other just as much as yourselves.

———————

I needed to find horses.

I saw an ad in a local newspaper for part-time barn help. I went to meet with Lee, the owner of the Van Nostern Arabian Horse Ranch. She was a tall, slender woman, fiftyish, with short graying hair. The ranch was pretty big, housing around forty horses. It sat atop a small, grassy hill with the Rocky Mountains in the distance like some stone fence line made long ago by giants.

"You took a job where you have to shovel horse manure?" Mom said to me on the phone. She had paid for my college education.

"Well, I'm also going to be mowing the grass." That should justify it.

"Why? If you need extra money —"

"Money has nothing to do with it."

"Then why do you want to pick through horse manure every day?"

"I just want to be around it."

"Horse crap?"

"No, the horses. I need to be around the horses."

"Well…okay. Alright. Just let me know if you need anything."

I could have told her I was going to train to be a Navy SEAL, and after some down-to-earth advice, she would have made sure I had enough hand grenades and some night-vision goggles.

I kept the job at the school and started working for the Van Nostern ranch a few days a week, as well. I spent the morning with the kids, popped myself full of hay fever meds and headed to the ranch through mid-afternoon, then made it back for after-school with the kids. I also started taking riding lessons with Lee whenever I could.

I really enjoyed cleaning the stalls and paddocks. I always hung out with the horses for a while after I finished. Each one of them was different in how they interacted with me. I loved it, just getting to be around them. I watched them as they fed, played, and rested.

One day I was pushing a wheelbarrow full of manure across the yard when I saw Lee's daughter Pam saying hello to her horse, Spring Break, a chestnut Arabian mare. The horse was in a paddock with a few others, and Pam was talking to her over the fence. I couldn't hear what she was saying. Her back was to me, so I couldn't even see her expression. But I could see Spring Break's. The mare came walking over to Pam, and as she got closer, her pace picked up. Pam didn't reach to pat or touch her horse's head right off, like most humans seemed to do, she actually just stood there. It was as though she was having a conversation with…another person. The horse wasn't a person—I knew that. It was just Pam seemed to be treating the conversation with the same respect.

They stood together for a while, Pam talking, Spring Break listening. Or maybe Spring Break was talking and Pam was listening. Pam stepped through the fence to stand with her horse. She then walked toward the other horses in the paddock and Spring Break followed as Pam looked their legs and bodies over, the daily routine of checking for anything that needed attention. After a stop at the water tank to make sure it was full, Pam stepped back outside the fence and then brought some hay out for each horse that they gratefully accepted. And there it was again, that content look in the horses' eyes and that meditative sound of their eating.

The whole interaction was subtle, profound. A daily occurrence yet infinitely special. Taking care of horses must bring such fulfillment, I thought. What a place to find yourself in life. I wondered if I would ever have the responsibility. I wondered if I would ever have the honor.

The responsibility of taking care of a bunch of kids, though?

I was not finding any honor in that.

I looked constantly for another job, and if somebody had offered me anything, I was ready to leave those kids in the dust. I tried to keep them corralled and keep them from killing themselves—and me. I tried to do the best I could, but it wasn't working. Everything was so scattered and disorganized. When they got unruly, I pleaded with them to stop but they wouldn't. And then, always, eventually…

"What is going on in here!"

Mr. Ray and his form-fitting sweaters would get them to stop immediately. The kids didn't mess around with that dude.

One day he pulled me aside. "Listen," he started. "These kids can't be running around like they are. You better shape up or things are going to have to change around here. Understand?"

The children were concerned after I "got in trouble." It seemed my patience and dedication to them had indeed helped them to open up, and they seemed to be starting to like me. That made me feel good. Then suddenly a dodgeball flew out of nowhere and nailed me in the crotch.

I wanted to do well at this job for them, but how could I when I didn't have any confidence in what I was doing? It led to them not having any confidence in me either. I'd thought the position would be fun and easy, but now I just wanted out. I wasn't enjoying the experience, and even worse, I thought I was letting the kids down. They needed someone *better*.

One day I was cleaning Major Headline's stall. He was a young Arabian colt and full of energy in all directions. As I mucked, he started to push into me. I politely asked him to stop. This just seemed to make him push harder. When I tentatively pushed back a little, his ears went flat back against his head and his tail swished, making a sharp, whip-like sound.

"Look out!" said Lee. She moved past me with an assertive posture and clapped her hands loudly all while staring at Headline straight in the eyes. He immediately backed up by his own choice. His ears came forward, and then he lowered his head to Lee and blinked repeatedly. Then, for some reason, he started softly licking his lips and chewing as if eating. It looked relaxing for him. After a moment of silence Lee softened her assertive posture and started talking to the horse in a quiet way while patting him on his withers.

The whole thing looked like Headline was saying, *I'm sorry*.

"You have to have boundaries," Lee said. "If he is trying to push you around, you need to let him know that's not acceptable. It's best when you can see a behavior when it's still just a thought in his mind. Use enough body language and energy to get his attention, then enough energy to inspire knew, good thoughts."

The horse was melting into her hands.

"Horses are more relaxed when they know what the boundaries are," she went on. "They *want* structure and guidance. When it's not there, they think they have to fill it in." She hugged the colt. "It doesn't help Headline to learn how to push people. Horses like that get bad reputations and get passed around. Helping him to respect boundaries is first and foremost in *his* best interest."

She had me try it. I tried to make Headline step back away from me, but he didn't respond at all. Lee laughed.

"You have the body language right," she said warmly, "but right now Headline sees it as just an empty shell. You have to believe it on the inside. Bring up your energy and believe in yourself, that he *will* move for you."

"How do I do that," I asked, "when I don't feel like I know what I'm doing?"

"You just find a beginning. A small place to start from, like with me helping you here. That gets the ball rolling. Once you get it kind of right and get some good results, then your confidence will grow, and you'll have something to build from."

I nodded my head and sneezed twice.

"Are you allergic?" asked Lee.

"Hay fever," I replied, like it didn't matter.

I started to get to know the kids better, and we became, well, closer. They really seemed to like me and my devotion to playing games with them and helping them with homework, but the craziness still prevailed with yelling and the screaming drowning out everything else. One day while playing dodgeball in the gym there was another breakdown. The whole gang was involved in the game, and it was organized. Then there was an argument between two kids. While dealing with it I lost track of the others and they started running around. I pleaded to keep the game going but no one listened. The rest of the afternoon was mayhem. I resorted to threatening punishment. *Get back in here or I'll tell your parents about this when they get here!* It was an empty threat and the kids all knew it. Again Mr. Ray had to step in, and I got yet another talking to.

When Lee was with Headline she had been assertive and definitive to get his attention, but she was also completely calm and relaxed, unemotional and non-threatening. She knew without a doubt what she was doing was going to work. And the whole time she had the feeling of being Headline's friend, of being on his side, even while correcting him.

When I yelled at the kids I was frustrated and angry. I hated how it felt.

It was on my mind constantly while cleaning the horse stalls. I would finish early and then sit somewhere and just observe the horses, watching closely how they interacted and moved each other. I would get lost in them, most of the time without them even knowing I was there.

The black stallion always knew when I was watching him, though.

He was The Prairie Drumbeat, a four-year-old Arabian stallion. He noticed every time I walked into the barn. Standing there, close to the bars, his eyes intently followed me. And I could feel it. I would get a feeling while I was mucking out a stall and I would turn to look and there he would be, silently watching me. There was something heavy about it. But every time I approached his stall he backed up into the corner. Still staring at me. I wanted to say something to him but didn't know what. I almost felt…unworthy. I'd heard he was a lot to handle and didn't let anyone get near him.

There was an air about Drumbeat. A pull to his gaze. And it was a look I had seen somewhere before.

4 | Guided

IT CAN BE hard to talk. To say what we feel and get it to come out right so someone understands.

Whenever we are in the presence of another, be it human or animal, we are communicating. We're always talking. We focus so much on words, though, that we don't feel our eyes, our breathing, our subtle body language, or our energy and what it's saying, and rarely do we notice all this in the one we are communicating with. We don't communicate purposefully with our whole being, nor see and feel the whole being in front of us.

Horses do, though.

Imagine a being who has spent fifty-five million years communicating primarily through energy, feel, body language, smell, touch…and then lastly through vocalization. That's horses. And it enables them to see and feel all of who we are and what we are saying, both consciously and subconsciously. Where you look matters. Your posture and movement matters. Your breathing matters. And yes, your smell matters. How we feel gives off a specific scent and horses can pick it up.

And while we are connecting with a horse through all this, there may come a time when we ask him to follow us. Why? Because we know when to cross the road and he doesn't. In the human world where horses are domesticated, for their safety and well-being, it's in their best interest to follow our lead when we ask. And how we do this matters very much.

So much of leading horses is done through varying levels of dominance based on a one-dimensional relationship where it's only about what the human wants from the horse. People focus solely on getting the body of the horse to do what they want by applying degrees of physical pressure and releasing the pressure once the horse has reacted as desired. It's a force applied from the outside-in, causing a discomfort, however light or firm, that the horse then tries to figure out how to get away from. All the horse is doing is moving his body to alleviate an annoyance or unpleasantness we are causing.

Would we do this with a human? A child? If no, then why is it okay to do it with a horse? The answer, invariably, is that we may think horses are lesser than humans in some way. But do horses think they are lesser? If you have seen a horse struggling for his life, you have seen he wants to live just as much as any human.

What if we could have a mental conversation with a horse instead of just a physical one? What if we could understand each other at a whole new level? What if they liked working with us? What if they looked for our guidance? All we would then have to do is convey to them what we wanted, and they would take care of the "doing it" from there.

It begins with having a feel for the horse's attention. So much of our struggle, both human and horse, comes from a lack of attention. If the horse has his two eyes and two ears on us, his "best try" to do what we are asking is usually not far behind. From there we need to develop the ability to use our own energy and body language in a non-intimidating and non-threatening way that is designed to get the horse's attention and then communicate, and inspire the horse to take seriously, what we are asking. But we need to have a feel for the horse's thoughts and feelings and connect with him there, first, as all movement of his body is just a result of those thoughts and feelings. That's where we will most easily recognize his "best try," because it's different in every horse. Knowing what a horse's best try feels and looks like is of the utmost importance. We don't have to worry about getting any-thing completely correct right off, for if we have his best try, he'll find the right answer eventually.

To get the horse's attention and to ensure his best try, our energy sometimes needs to be light, sometimes steady, and sometimes rising. The intention is to bring our energy *up* but not *at* the horse. The horse very much knows the difference—one is communicating to him, the other can be taken as a physical threat.

Once we have the horse's try, the timing of how we acknowledge it becomes very important. Sometimes we must give a complete release of our request, sometimes just a half-release to let the horse know he is on the right track while we ask for him to continue. When we really come together with the horse, there is no need to release to reward him; we just hold the feel of what we are asking until we are finished.

From there we move together, with us in the lead and the horse atten-tive and inspired to raise or lower his own energy by matching our energy, following our body language for guidance. This is where both human and horse have fun with it, above and below the surface.

We will never be able to control a horse's body better than he can him-self. But if he is seeking our guidance, if we have his best try, and if he *feels good* about it, then he will move in perfect focus, balance, and confidence of his own accord every single time.

This teaches us to ask ourselves what our motivation in life is. Are we just moving away from pressures, or are we seeking greater guidance?

Are we spending our days avoiding the dark, or are we following the light?

———————

We were playing another game of kickball. It was going well. Then a bit of arguing started, as it usually did. I noticed some of the kids getting bored. I could feel it coming. I had become sensitive to it.

The yelling broke out and kids started running around.

I saw the future. I would try to reorganize the kids to no avail, and then Mr. Ray would make his scheduled appearance. As I stood there, silent, knowing nothing good was coming, I realized my thinking was off. I was expecting it to go bad, waiting for it to go bad. *No.* I needed to do something. I needed to flip the script and inspire something positive to happen.

But everything I usually tried didn't work.

Then it hit me. It hit me like a dodgeball to the crotch.

I was the softness, the friend, but that was all I was. Mr. Ray was the firmness, the boss, but that was all he was.

I had the kids' friendship. I had overdosed on the friendship. But I had no leadership. So now I was going to have to overdose on that to get the balance I needed.

"EVERYBODY STOP RIGHT NOW!"

It felt good because I wasn't yelling *at* them. The energy went *up*, instead of *at* them. I got their attention in a serious way. This was going to stop *now*. It was unfortunate I had let the situation get this far, where I had to now make a stand. But the firmness was for their own good.

They stopped. Silence. Eyes on me.

Okay. I had their attention. And I wasn't angry or frustrated. I was clear and focused. I understood. I saw what I had to do, I knew how to do it, and knew it would work. And when you know all of this you are relaxed and patient.

"Here it is. You have two options," I said very directly. "The first one, I am going to take away your gym time, from here on out, and I am going to tell all your parents, one by one, how unruly you are. Or option number two, you guys listen to me, and we play a fun and organized game of kickball." I paused for a second, and then ended with, "Your choice…"

The kids looked at me. Something was different about this, they could tell.

"But I'm tired of kickball," whined Dylan.

"I will take that into consideration, Dylan, and tomorrow we'll play something different, but today kickball is the game."

"But I—"

"Enough!" I said definitively. "We *all* play kickball today. Understand?"

"Yes," said Dylan.

"Thank you," I replied.

We played. The game was organized and played almost in a business-like manner by the kids. At one point Doug and Amanda started fighting.

"Amanda, Doug, do I need to go get my buddy Mr. Ray to come in here and play kickball with us?" I said assertively but calmly.

They both stopped and shook their heads no.

"Because I will. I'll make him a team captain. And he kicks hard and throws hard. And he makes his team wear tight sweater uniforms. You guys want that?"

"No," they both said with hints of smiles.

"Okay then. Doug, you got tagged so you are out. Amanda, next time do not throw the ball so hard. Understand?"

They nodded their heads yes.

I did *not* let it get out of hand. It was a choice, a decision, to just not let it get out of hand. At the end of the game the kids quietly stood in a line in front of me with all eyes on me.

"That was great, guys. Thank you," I said as I walked up and down the line. "Answer me, yes or no: Do you all understand that you need to listen to me and do as I say, any time, all the time, every time, for this to go well and be fun for all of us?"

"Yes," the kids said together. I could see the thinking going on behind their eyes.

"Okay, then. Because guess what? I actually *want* to do what you want to do. I want to help you guys with your homework, I want to play games with you, I want you to learn new things, and I want you to have fun doing it all. I'm here for you. I want you to lead the way. But to do all this you have to listen to me and do as I say, because believe it or not, the rules are actually here to help you."

I could feel we were at a changing point. Something about this was going to stick. And I knew the perfect finish.

"And now we have time for a game of safe and organized dodgeball," I announced. "Except this game will be different. It will be all of you versus me. And if you win…you get a movie and pizza party this Friday after school."

Young faces lit up.

And so after school on Friday the kids excitedly ran into the cafeteria. They all sat eating pizza, and as I got the movie ready to play, I turned to them and asked a question: "Do you know why you got this pizza party?"

"Because we got along together," said Amanda.

"Because we played the game safely," said Sarah

"Because we listened to you," answered Sean.

"That's right, guys. Because it's really all about your safety and what is good for you. Not just today but for the long run. If you pay attention to me we'll have a lot of fun. You're all great kids and I want you to have a great time here. And to do that, you gotta follow my lead. Deal?"

"Yes!" they shouted.

Why do horses let us guide them? They are so big and powerful that if they didn't want to there would be nothing we could do about it.

The answer: because true leadership has nothing to do with size, strength, or power.

It wasn't about the kids and me waiting for them to change. They naturally wanted guidance and a sense of security. It was about me and what I was feeling and then thinking and then doing. I felt love for these kids. I wanted them to be safe and to be happy. I wanted to help them to listen and to learn, to be calm and to focus and to dream. To be excited about life.

And to do all of this I would have to lead.

At the end of my days at the ranch I would walk down the aisle of the barn and stop to see each horse. Most would say hello and show interest in me.

Not The Prairie Drumbeat though. He always backed away the moment I got close. The black Arabian stallion seemed to be a loner at an early age, ignoring my consistent attempts to make friends with him. But that gaze. It knew something.

I stood there in silence in front of his stall, staring at him. He stared back with that look. That look I had seen somewhere before. The light glimmered off his metallic coat. His eyes watched me from underneath his long forelock. I had an urge and before thinking about it could get in the way I opened the door.

He quickly positioned himself in the back right corner. His eyes locked on me. I walked in. I felt him watching me as I kept my eyes to the ground. He studied me, acutely aware of every movement, every thought. I stood still. I talked to him like I talked to all the horses. I sneezed twice. My medication was wearing off.

After a minute or so I heard his feet moving. He had taken a step toward me. Out of the corner of my eye I saw him stretching his neck to get his nose closer. He was interested. He took a cautious step forward, then another, until the whiskers of his nose were brushing against my shoulder.

Instead of moving to pat him, I just kept talking to him. After a moment I softly looked up at him. He raised his head cautiously. I smiled and lowered my eyes again, my shoulders. He then lowered his head and extended it out to me once more.

The colt's nose slowly rose until it was inches from mine. I could feel his breathing in warm and gentle puffs as his nostrils subtly flared along with them. I breathed back to him. We were exchanging breath…and something much bigger. What I was thinking mattered, too, and right then all I thought about was how happy I was to be where I was. Something told me the little things that were happening were a big deal to the horse in front of me.

Drumbeat took a few more steps to get closer. I reached up with my hand. He hesitated, then brought his nose to it, examining it, feeling it. I rubbed his upper lip and became lost in the bristly and fuzzy texture. The rubbing with my finger spoke to him in some way.

If I was calm in my presence and moved in a soft way that was sure of itself, he seemed to open up. I could then "give back" to him in some way. He would then give back to me, and in this…trust was forming. This was how it…worked. In a second, I saw our whole future relationship. It was like… like there was something there, something coming, and the black colt knew all about it, he was in on the secret, he *was* the secret and...

…I remembered where I had seen it before. That look in Drumbeat's eyes.

The two horses Ally was feeding in the barn the night we broke up.

"So how do you like it here?"

I turned around to see Lee and her daughter, Pam.

"Oh, I love it. Thanks so much for giving me the opportunity." Drumbeat stepped back into the corner again.

"You get along well with the horses," said Pam.

I looked at Drumbeat. "They're good to be around," I replied.

"And you seem to be really interested in them," said Lee.

"I am."

"Well, maybe we can help you there," she went on. "We have an apprentice trainer program. It's unpaid, like an internship. Most of our apprentices come from colleges with equine programs. But you seem to have a genuine feel for the horses."

The next morning after I finished before-school with the kids, I went to the ranch, and instead of mucking stalls, I got started as an apprentice trainer. I worked with Major Headline, the yearling stallion, and AA Nocturne, a twenty-year-old black stallion. Nocturne was the veteran, seen it all and done it all. He "filled in" for me, helping me learn. Headline, on the other hand, needed someone to fill in for him. He was young and needed help learning how to be led and how to find confidence within himself. Nocturne helped teach me, Headline helped me learn to teach.

"Slow him down, slow him down," said Pam as she watched while I "lunged" Nocturne in circles on a long line. He was running hard around me, and I kept getting the line mixed up in my hands and around my feet. Nocturne was just doing his own thing.

"Try to help him listen to you," said Pam.

"But he seems to know that I don't know what I'm doing."

"All you have to do is begin as simple as you can get it, like walking him in a circle on this line. Don't think it's this big mountain to climb; think about it like it's simple common sense. For instance, stop him, right now."

"Now?"

"Now."

I let out a deep breath and relaxed my posture and said, "Whoaaaa," while choking up on the line and giving Nocturne a feel on his halter that hopefully said stop. And he did.

"See? Look at that," said Pam. "You can get him to stop any time you want. That's a big thing. Now get him going again."

I asked Nocturne to go back out on the circle, and after me fumbling around for a while longer, he managed it at a walk.

"How will he know when he can fully trust me?" I asked.

"When you trust yourself. And that will come in time."

I knew Pam was trying to instill in me some deeper meaning to the horse-human relationship, but it was hard to take in while thirty feet of nylon lunge line was wrapping around my legs like a boa constrictor. All I needed now was Mr. Ray to come up behind me and tell me how awful I was doing.

"Every Monday I am going to put a quote on the wall and the name of the person who said it, and I will give you all a week to memorize the quote and the name. At the end of that week, I will ask one of you to recite the quote to me and tell me who said it."

The first quote for the kids came from preacher and author Leroy Brownlow: *A loud voice cannot compete with a clear voice no matter how loud it is.*

They got into it. They all went to work memorizing the words. They quizzed each other. They rooted for each other when I asked one of them to recite the quote.

I was finding balance and the program started to come together. I was patient and consistent with them, and they respected the boundaries I set. They listened to me the first time I said something or gave directions. They respected my rules, seeming to understand it was for their best interest, and when I corrected them, they understood the reasoning why. There was structure. And it was fun. I looked forward to spending time with them each day.

Somehow word got out because the program started growing. Soon there were so many kids signing up that the school hired an assistant for me. Karen was in her mid-twenties and had the look of an honest and happy person. She was warm and caring, anybody could see it. She was married and had just moved to the area.

Karen was a natural. She had the same way with the kids that I tried to have. It wasn't about giving the kids an answer or just making them do something the way we wanted, but instead helping them to find their own way to an answer. Teaching them how to make their own good decisions. It was great to see their excitement when they found their way. It was their triumph. That built their self-confidence and had them wanting to learn more.

My riding lessons with Lee moved forward on a mare named Kassari. We focused on dressage—training and riding precise movements of the horse's body—but sometimes we would work on Western reining, which consisted of circles, spins, and stops. Lee was really into it and made every second of the lesson count.

"Think soft and free eyes," instructed Lee. "Where your eyes go the horse feels. So look where you want to go, and see the ground you will be traveling to get there, and look to the horse when you need to, just keep your chin up while your eyes take it all in. That will keep your ears, shoulders, and hips aligned and your seat balanced with the horse. Think soft eyes and breathe. The horse can feel your breathing. Breathe in, relaxing your jaw, with deep breaths that take their time. Your eyes and your breathing unite the ride."

Back with the kids, Karen was working out great. She was very fun, and more than that, she was not just another set of eyes watching over the kids. She had something to offer. She was there to make a difference in their lives.

We instituted what we called the "Green Point Chart." We put it on the wall with the kids' names, and whenever they did a "good deed," they would get a green point beside their name. Karen and I believed in letting the kids be in charge of their own actions and learning to be responsible for consequences of those actions, but we also set up opportunities for all the kids to be successful. Soon the children were jumping from their seats to hold the door for each other or to help classmates with homework.

We had been using the Green Point Chart for about a month when one of the kids, Sean, asked if he could talk with me.

"If I get any more green points," he said, "could you give them to one of the other kids? And could you not tell that I did it?"

I looked at him in a serious way. Not as an adult looking at a kid but as a person who admired another person. "Why do you want to do this?" I asked.

"I don't know. It would feel good to me."

I smiled. "Sean, I'm impressed. That's what this is all about. Doing good deeds and being kind, not just because of how it makes other people feel, but because of how it makes *you* feel."

Parents started mentioning how happy they were with the program, how their kids were telling them stories over dinner of how much they enjoyed it. Some children even asked their parents to pick them up later so they could stay longer after school.

I forgot being with the kids was a job. I would have been there playing the games with them by choice. If someone offered me a different gig with more money, benefits, better hours, even bartending in downtown Denver...

Sorry. I'm with the kids.

5 | The Fabled Demons

"ARE YOU SCARED?" someone asked the woman who was about to ride a horse for the first time.

"Of course," she said. "Deep down somewhere, we're all afraid of this."

Fear is natural, ever-present, swirling around inside, and rising up from time to time. It's not *if* we get scared, because we will. It is how we react to it. What we choose to do in the face of our fear is what we have control of and, in the end, what can lead to our greatest triumphs. Fear, like pain, is a guide. It highlights where we may need to slow down and have help. Where we can go deeper in our understanding of ourselves, our horses, and the world around us.

Fear is here to help us.

Horses are much bigger than us, and because of this, we are naturally on guard around them. We think size equals strength. It's sometimes hard for us to have confidence when around a thousand-pound animal, let alone ride it. It's hard to trust our horses and even harder to trust ourselves—that we will always know what to do.

But from a horse's perspective, *we* are more dangerous than they are. To them, size has nothing to do with strength. If it did then draft horses would rule the herds. It would also render horses untamable. If horses thought in terms of who is stronger, no human could ride a horse.

A horse lives in his mind. A horse senses the strength of presence, the intent within—what the mind is capable of, not the body. And don't we humans think that way as well? We're afraid of dangerous situations, both physically (heights, speed) and mentally (dishonesty, broken hearts). The big difference with animals, and especially horses, is they don't hide fear. They don't pretend it isn't there. They don't get mad if someone confronts them about their fears. They don't deny it or feel weak for being scared. They make no apologies for showing their fear.

There is no reason to ever get mad or frustrated with any human or any horse when they are scared. The focus should be on how to help. We can do this in many ways, but an important beginning is that they trust us. This means starting as slowly as possible with easy situations that build that trust, making sure there is no intimidation in our work, that they don't feel threatened, and that they feel good in mind and body about it all.

Horses have a great reputation for being a flight animal, but are they really any more scared than other animals? Than humans? If you watch horses in the wild, or domesticated horses in a field, paddock, or stall, how often do you see them get scared and spook? Yet when we work with them or ride them they can seem to jump at any little thing. Why is this?

The answer lies in the anxiety and tension that we and the horses can carry while working *together*. Imagine yourself in the horse's place with a halter on your head and the lead line in a human's hands; with a bit in your mouth connected to reins in a human's hands; being ridden by a human while legs and possibly spurs apply pressure to your sides. Add to this the possibility that you, like many horses, might be in physical pain somewhere, and this creates additional stress that sits right there under the surface, building up…looking to be released. And when you suddenly notice something out of place or hear a loud noise or see an unexpected move-ment—well, you release that stress in a spook or jump or bolt. And when you get scared that causes the human to get scared.

When we look deeply, human fears aren't all that different than a horse's. We carry a lot of stress, too, that sits waiting to be released in some way. And just like horses, most of the time we will try to avoid that which makes us afraid. But the cycle of our fears showing themselves gives us an opportunity to understand them. And they will keep coming back around until we face them. Some breakthroughs take years, others just days.

Just think of what your fears are.

Now think of someone, human or horse, who helps you get through them. You are tied to them for the rest of your life.

Bonded.

———————————

My riding lessons were getting more complex.

Lee was watching every detail. I first learned to ride with a loose rein, and now I was working on having the correct contact on the reins. *Hands that pass softness back and forth to the horse. Your eyes, seat, and leg bake the cake; your contact on the reins is the icing on it.*

One day I was trying to get Kassari to "bend like a banana" as we were riding to the left. My instinct was to use more rein. What little rein I started with led to more, and pretty soon, I was basically pulling her head in the direction of the turn.

Lee slowed me down.

"Remember, the rein is the final touch," she started. "It's not what makes the horse turn. Think about all the communication you have available. Your eyes look where you want to go. That causes you to shift your weight, which the horse feels and it takes them in that direction. If needed, use your outside leg to urge the horse into the direction of travel. Use your inside leg forward toward the girth for support so the horse doesn't fall inside. These two leg cues will balance off each other with the outside leg leading the way. This will put the horse in a balanced position for the turn. Then the inside rein softly guides the horse's vision, just slightly, and the outside rein stays steady, supporting, and controls how far the horse bends. And you have a beautiful turn with the horse using his whole body in a strong and balanced way."

You ride from back to front: seat and leg first to generate energy and impulsion and then seat and leg layered on top of that for directional guidance. Then comes the rein contact, a soft feel for guiding the thoughts of the horse, helping the horse to use his whole body in the best way possible.

"The reins work in conjunction with the legs in diagonal pairs," said Lee. "The outside leg works with the inside rein for directional guidance, the inside leg works with the outside rein for support, and this keeps the horse balanced."

At the local library I was reading or watching anything about horses I could find. There were days when I would go and study the horse books all day as I furiously scribbled down notes. I started to condense certain training ideas into one line sentences I could remember:

The right attitude first, then good horse care, then working with them.

You yourself must first have the qualities you hope to teach your horse.

Relax your mind, your body will follow.

You can't make yourself relax, but you can make yourself breathe, and if you breathe you will relax.

You can't have two leaders when trying to move as one—someone has to lead.

If you get lost or frustrated, stop and go back to something you and the horse do well together, then work your way up again— retreat to make progress.

One day I was leading Nocturne out to the hot-walker and I stopped dead in my tracks. I had run out of hay fever medication a week ago. There was no sneezing. No congestion. No itchy, watery eyes.

Something in me was changing.

———————————

It was five-thirty in the afternoon and the teachers had gone home for the night. I walked slowly through the empty school with four foam dodgeballs in my hands. Everything was quiet. I came to an intersection and stealthily peeked down each hallway. Nothing. I turned around and saw Kyle and Doug sprinting the other way. They were making a break for it. I went running after them, throwing balls at them rapid-fire style.

"Gooze" was a game that Karen, the kids, and I made up that could *only* be played after all the teachers had gone home. One "hunter" had to search the school for all the "runners" and try to tag them with a dodgeball before they made it to a circle "safe zone" that was taped in the middle of the floor in the cafeteria.

A game Mr. Ray would love, I was sure.

What allowed us to be able to play this game was the mutual respect we had. I trusted these kids now. I knew they would follow the rules of the game and not mess around in the school and get into trouble while they were out of sight. Not because I told them not to, but because they understood that it wasn't cool to do so.

One round Karen and I were the runners while all the kids searched for us. We hid behind the curtains on the stage in the gymnasium and waited.

"So how did you end up in Colorado working here?" she whispered.

"Well…" I peered out toward the door, looking for hunters. "My girl-friend broke up with me and I loved her but it was obvious that I was not ready to be in the relationship and then I lost my job and then I went broke and through all this I realized there was something missing inside me and I met horses for the first time and felt something I had never felt so I took off west."

Whoops. Honesty. When people asked me why I came out west I would usually just say I wanted to see the land.

She didn't flinch. "So you were hurting and felt lost. Now you've found a path and you're following it, putting yourself back together in a new way."

I didn't know how to respond, so I said, "Yup."

"Well, it was obvious to me that you're searching for something. It was also obvious that you feel you are onto it, and you won't stop until you find it."

I stared at her, wondering what else she knew.

"Look out, it's Sarah!" Karen said, pointing to the other end of the stage where one of the kids was looking behind the curtains. We made a break for it and ran into a barrage of dodgeballs. Karen made it to safety. I went down. Another shot to the crotch.

Later, after all the kids had gone home, Karen and I sat in the cafeteria talking.

"So, what was this woman like?" she asked.

"Allison? Well, she was…natural. Authentic. Definitely herself. Yeah, she had found herself and she was ready to go forward with it."

"And you hadn't?"

I paused and thought about that for a moment.

"There is something in me that…I never knew was there," I finally replied. "Some sort of...discontentment? I don't know, maybe I did feel it now and then. But now I feel it for sure and there's no turning back."

"Turning back from what?"

"Trying to find...the contentment."

"Okay. And where are you going to look? Where is the next place?" she asked.

"As crazy as it seems, I think it's Hollywood."

"Hollywood?" Karen smiled and shook her head. "I do not see you in Hollywood."

"Agreed. I don't either. But that's the plan."

It was the plan. But I was scared.

How many horses were there in Hollywood?

———————

At the Van Nostern Ranch, a new horse named Booker arrived. He had been brought to the ranch in the hopes he could be calmed down. Apparently, he had become very hard to handle after an accident.

The dun Quarter Horse jumped when he first saw me, and then backed away and hid his face in the dark corner of the stall. He paced back and forth while keeping an unblinking eye on me. It was a look from a horse I hadn't seen yet—wild and primal fear.

Lee and Pam made a call. A man arrived in an old, broken-down truck. He got out wearing chaps, boots, and a black cowboy hat. I put him in his late thirties. He walked into the barn slowly with calm intent. His hat and chaps were scuffed and scraped from past work. The eyes and face, the same. And he was quiet like Seth, the cowboy I met on the trail ride in the Black Hills.

I watched as he walked down toward the barn to where Booker's stall was. I wondered what he was going to do. How could someone help a horse that was so far gone into his own fear?

During my riding lessons I focused on cantering. I was in love with the movement and all the subtleties of it. How you first pick up into it and feel the strong movement of the horse and your hair blows back and the sound of the wind is in your ears and you are flying. How the horse's head dips up and down as he stretches forward, mane streaming back, and the perfect sound of the hooves in each stride.

At the school we were still in the right rhythm with the kids. They were great. They looked to our lead, and they looked to our guidance. We still had outbursts now and then and the occasional temper tantrum, but Karen and I just stayed calm and didn't add any negative energy to the situation, and of course didn't let the kids' unbalanced behavior accomplish anything. And at the end, we would always be there for them to talk, to explain something, or encourage them to figure out a better way. A lot of times they just had to get something out of their systems, and once out, they were back with us in a positive way.

"I think it's getting time for me to move on," I said to Bart.

We were hiking in the Utah Canyonlands. We had set up camp and were watching the sunset from a giant rock that was as smooth as a porcelain plate. It sat in the middle of a large grass field surrounded by a circle of the towering rock needles the Canyonlands were famous for. The needles had an opening in them to the west, giving the rock, the grass field, and the needles the aura of being constructed for this exact purpose—an amphitheater for honoring the sunset.

"You really gonna head to Hollywood?" asked Bart.

"I got those old screenplays I wrote. Always wondered about them. And at some point, I need to think about the future. So it makes sense while I am out here."

"Well, I'm with you on it all. You know you got that."

"Yeah. Thanks, man."

We went quiet for a while. The way sunsets slow down everything.

"How much do you still think about her?" Bart then said.

I thought of the best way to answer. "She's always there. Sometimes I think about her for hours. Sometimes she's just there behind the scenes. A reflection. But Ally is always there in some way."

"Do you ever think of the possibility of getting back together with her?"

"I don't know, man," I said. "When it comes to that stuff, I just don't trust my instincts anymore. Every woman I have ever felt anything for is no longer in my life."

"Makes you afraid, right?" remarked Bart. "Afraid you'll get hurt again. Afraid you might hurt her. Afraid you lost something that may have been right. Afraid you'll never find something that will be right."

"Yeah." I looked out at the sunset blazing across the sky. "Ally once told me that relationships are hard. That they take hard work and sacrifice to keep. I told her I didn't think that was all the way right. That if you love someone it should be easy to be with them. That in the end there isn't any hard work or sacrifice if you really love someone."

"You still believe that?"

"I think relationships…they're not about what I thought they were. I think there's everything in them, they hold all the journey of a life. And I don't think they're about some sort of connection that will help take away the pains of living. I think they dig and pull and peel until we're…exposed, showing all of ourselves."

"And that can definitely lead to a lot of fear and fighting," said Bart, laughing.

"This whole thing, it feels like there's something that's been asleep inside me that's waking up," I said. "Something that my soul wants to bring to the surface. And it won't come without this heart pain."

"We all have a soul that wants to continuously lead, die, be re-born, and lead the way again," Bart offered thoughtfully. "It's tough, though, because where it takes us doesn't make sense sometimes, at least not as to the plans of our life we thought we had. But you gotta follow it. You gotta make your way through the fear of losing all the structure and safety and security you thought you had. Of who you thought you were."

We watched the sun lower itself some more.

"So...do you think there is a chance for you and Allison ever again?" he asked again.

I wanted to answer. I wanted to have something to say on it. I wanted to have an idea of what the future may hold.

"I will see her again someday," I said. "I'm pretty sure of it."

And the sun went down.

A few days later the phone rang. It was Karen. She had never called me at home before. We joked at first and then I expected her to get to some reason she called but she never did. We ended up just talking on the phone for an hour. After we said goodbye, I sat on the kitchen counter holding the phone. *What was that?* We were becoming good friends, so I guessed it was just a friendly phone call. She was married.

I went back to getting myself dinner.

The next day Karen and I were walking out to our cars after the morning session, and there was a rose on the windshield of my car. I picked it up and looked at her.

"Have a nice day," she said with a smile.

She drove away as I sat there in the Grand Prix. "She just left a rose on the windshield for me," I said aloud. "What does *that* mean?"

And then a couple days later when we were leaving after the afternoon session she said, "I just wanted to tell you how good you look today."

"Oh, yeah, thanks," I replied, going out of my way to pretend it was the most normal thing in the world for her to compliment me.

I asked Bart what he thought.

"She digs you, man."

"But she has a husband," I quickly replied.

"Yeah, and she gave you a rose."

I looked at the rose that was now in a vase in the kitchen.

"So what are you going to do?" said Bart.

"I don't think there's anything *for* me to do. I just wonder about her, you know? She's a great woman in so many ways. Smart and funny, great with the kids. And she really pays attention to things. She looks out for you. She lets you know she believes in you. That's rare."

Bart grinned and shook his head.

I was down to my last week in Colorado.

I had gotten permission to use a bus to take the kids on a field trip to the Van Nostern Ranch. Lee and Pam were great as they talked with the group and introduced them to the different horses. Lee was having such a good time she saddled up a horse and started giving pony rides. The kids loved it. As they walked through the barns, all the horses hung their heads out to say hello. Children that were thought to be high-strung became relaxed around the horses. The horses that were thought to be high-strung stood relaxed and polite as the kids patted their noses. What did "high-strung" even mean, anyway? Did the kids or horses know they were high-strung? Or was it just a label from someone who wanted them to be a different way?

On my last day at the school the kids had a party for me. There were cakes, pies, and cupcakes that the parents made, and the kids gave me cards and gifts. I'd made cards for all of them, with a specific message written to each kid. We partied a bit, destroyed a piñata, and then sat down for some cake. It was loud, messy, and out of control. Just like the old days.

After the cake I stood up and got everyone's attention. "Guys, I would like to say something."

The children sat in front of me. I had their complete attention. Innocent eyes looked up to me. Behind them stood Karen.

"Thank you," I said. "Thanks for this party. I can't believe you did all this for me." I then paused. This was going to be harder than I thought.

"I guess I would like to start off by saying…there are a lot of things about you that, well, that I am…NOT going to miss!" They all started laughing. "I will not miss Dylan getting locked in the janitor's closet during Gooze. I will not miss being the 'one' in the ten-on-one water fights. And I certainly will not miss driving home in soggy socks after the water fights. I will not miss helping you with algebra problems that I do not even remotely understand. And most of all, I will NOT miss getting yelled at by Mr. Ray!"

The kids all laughed along with me.

"And then, guys, well…then there are the things about you I will miss. You've taught me so much and I have had just as much fun here as you have. I'm going to miss all the games we played together, especially Gooze. I'm going to miss seeing you do so well in the quote game and on the Green Point Chart, and seeing you being such great friends to each other. And pizza and movie Fridays—they were the best, I sure will miss them."

I looked down for a moment. Then I looked back up, ready to continue.

"Each and every one of you is amazing. And you are going to go on and do amazing things in life. You're great kids. But more than that, you have become great friends. And that is what I'm gonna miss the most. I'll miss my friends."

It was getting to me. I looked at Karen standing in the background. She was tearing up.

"And I guess I have to say thanks to Karen for helping put this party together."

I walked over to her like I was going to hug her...then instead picked up a bowl of Jell-O and went to dump it over her head. She saw it coming and tried to block it. Jell-O went flying all over both of us. The kids all jumped up in laughter.

Suddenly the children's laughter stopped. Karen got a very serious look on her face and motioned behind me. I turned around...and there was Mr. Ray.

The respect he demanded enveloped the room. He stood there looking at me the same way he had since I'd first started running around his school, and now he had caught me once again. I prepared for the tight-sweatered sheriff to take me down.

"I hear you're leaving," he said sternly.

"Yes, Mr. Ray, I am. This is my last day," I said as Jell-O slid down my neck.

"Well…I just wanted to wish you good luck. The kids will miss you, and… well… good job." He seemed almost embarrassed. I think he almost even smiled. Almost. "And this cafeteria is going to be cleaned spotless, right?"

"Yes, sir, Mr. Ray, of course."

The last thing Karen and the kids had for me was a photo book of pictures Karen had taken over the last months. On the inside cover there were notes written to me by the kids, the parents, the teachers, and even Mr. Ray.

There was also a letter addressed to me:

This letter is to thank you for all your hard work during your time spent at Northeast Elementary. It is with your dedication and desire an excellent program has been built for the children. You can be assured that the children have benefited from the time you have spent with them. You have left your mark on a community, and that is not something easily achieved.

You will be missed but what you are about to embark on sets an example to every child, parent, and co-worker you have met. You are chasing your dream, and we don't think there is anything more important or courageous than that. You told us that we don't owe you anything, but in actuality, we owe you everything. It is with people like you we strive to give children dreams. What better example could we have? You can rest assured we are all with you on your journey, and if you ever need anything, please let us know. Thanks for the time.

Sincerely,
The Sunrise, Sunset Program at Northeast Elementary School

I remembered when I wanted nothing more than to give up and get out of that school. All the frustration. I had no control. I didn't know what to do. Then I found out what to do and how to do it, and I worked at it, a little at a time.

And now I was having one of the best days of my life.

———————

Saturday night came and we were in the heart of Denver for my last night out on the town. Bart and a few other friends were there, and Karen had come out as well.

I was in the middle of everybody until somehow it ended up Karen and I alone. Funny how that happens, how it gravitates to that. Fight it though you may. She started asking more questions about what I saw for my future.

I tried to steer the conversation toward something else, but she kept finding a way to bring it back to me.

We sat side by side on a wooden bench away from everybody. It was packed and there were people standing all around us, so maybe it wasn't that we were away from everybody, we just didn't notice anybody. We talked. She intently stared into my eyes. I found myself being insanely truthful like I was jumping on the moment to purge myself of things needing to be said out loud. At one point I thought she was moving closer to me. I had been keeping an eye on the expanse of wood between us and concluded it was only my imagination. I felt her leg brush up against mine and then it stayed there, pressed against me, and I glanced down at what had been the space between us and whereas before I could see a foot of fine-crafted mahogany, now I could not. All there was to see was her thigh, in tan pants, against my thigh, causing a steady electrical pulse to radiate through my leg.

I did not want this. I wanted it to go away for I knew the only thing that could come of it was pain. *Come on! Why?* I had come to the West to rebuild. This was a blatant disregard for that. My soul was in an uproar.

"There's something I was thinking of telling you," she said. "Something I *need* to tell you."

I looked at her, telling her with my eyes not to say it. *Don't say it.*

I got up and went to the bathroom. I looked into the mirror, the way you look into a bathroom mirror when in the middle of some crazy life experience. The craziness is still out there, out in the bar or the living room or wherever, but you get that little quiet moment to be alone and look into the mirror, into your own eyes, to see where you're at.

You can't make yourself relax, but you can make yourself breathe, and if you breathe you will relax.

I started to just breathe, and I let my mind calm down. And in the next instant, I was thinking about horses.

Horses will not pretend, will not say things the wrong way and will not lie. Horses are no different from the inside to the outside. Their feelings and actions are one and the same. There is no filter between how horses feel and how they act. This holds us to a higher standard of communicating and living when we are around them.

All Karen was doing was communicating. She was communicating her feelings, hiding nothing, the same inside and out. That's all. She was just being…honest. And all I needed to focus on was my own thoughts and my own actions. The only thing I was truly in control of. All I needed to do was be honest back.

———————

I woke up early the next morning. I walked out onto the patio. The morning was chilly but with a fresh sun in a cloudless blue sky it was all just perfect. I breathed in the pure Colorado air and thought about the night before.

There was an email from Karen. She said she couldn't get her mind off me, that no matter what she was doing that morning, there I was. I started writing an email back. I liked being around her and the way she made me feel. She saw something in me that I needed someone to see, for someone to confirm it was there, or something.

But I did not talk about any of that in the email. What was going on was not about me, it was about her, and I couldn't encourage any of this. Instead I talked about how great a person she was, how terrific she was with the kids, how much potential I thought she had, and how I thought she seriously needed to sit down and talk with her husband. She was trying to communicate that there were some things missing in her life and she was looking for them elsewhere.

Later that night I received another email from her. She asked me to stop by and see her and the kids one last time. She went on to say if I didn't want to she would understand.

The next day I went to the school after all the kids had left. There was an art to saying goodbye and the party had been the perfect one with them. I walked into the room and there was Karen. We talked about the kids, but slowly the talk turned into something different. She moved closer, and pretty soon her head was on my shoulder. I put my arms around her and we hugged.

Tears formed in the corners of her eyes, and when the weight became too much they fell and coasted down her face, leaving a clear trail as if to prove they had been there.

"I never thought I would be like this," she said, choked up.

"Karen, you are a good, honest person. Maybe you just need to think about what you are really attracted to here and think about your relationships and what you need in them. What you're looking for."

"I know," she replied quietly. "There's some things I need to figure out about myself and my relationship. You just kinda threw me for a loop."

I reached into my pocket and took out a little piece of a branch, a twig no more than three inches long, that I'd broken off a tree while I was with my father. I must have been around ten years old when Dad and I were carrying a canoe through the woods to this little pond to go fishing. As we were walking, I casually reached up and snapped off the tiny end of a tree branch and put it in my pocket. Now I was giving it to her. I told her the story of it, what it symbolized, how it was something to keep to remind you of a time and place.

The sky was hard rain dark as I drove out of Colorado. This was the second time in less than a year I had lit out of a place like I was now, packing everything I could and driving away. Pretty soon it was nothing but the plains again stretching forever to either side of the gray pavement. The rain came at intervals.

I was scared.

What in the world was I doing driving to Hollywood?

It was time to move on from Colorado, yes, and I had those screenplays, yes, but…*the horses.*

I needed a future, though. A future with financial security. My friends: steady jobs with benefits and retirement plans. Me: a checking account with two thousand dollars in it. I had to do this, I had to focus on my future. The horses had to wait.

I thought about my last day at the Van Nostern Ranch. I went into the barn and said goodbye to Nocturne, Major Headline, and Prairie Drumbeat. They looked at me the way they always had, like they knew what I was thinking. I thanked them for all they had done for me, and as I walked away, they stood watching me. Drumbeat with that same heavy stare, like he knew more about me than I did. As I looked back one last time, he whinnied. And then another horse called out. They were all standing at the front of their stalls looking at me.

These horses, in their eyes, I felt they had a sense of mankind and how we are searching for something.

Horses know what is going on, I thought.

6 | Getting Closer

HORSES' BODIES ARE works of art, and once they begin connecting with us they are amazingly kind in how they allow us to guide how that body moves. Whether it be while completely free, with halter and lead rope, in long-lines, or playing games and performing tricks, there are always adventures to be had, with all of it adding to the depth of how we *know* each other.

We can think of it like this: When you have a good friend, you go on adventures together. You explore your town, and when you have seen all of it, you are then drawn to explore the next town over. Who better to do this with than our horse friends? The work we first do with them is like our hometown, and when we get bored there, we venture to a new town, with new work. That's all we need to see working with horses as—the current place we are exploring with them, and the future places we can go to, like riding and all its different forms, if we like.

It's natural to be curious about the world. But curiosity can turn to fear when pressure and stress surround horse and human. We don't want to be scared and we don't want horses to be scared. Seeing them scared, scares us. So we try and force them to not be scared and this then turns into a heightened anxiety and tension whenever we are in unfamiliar territory.

One of my favorite things to do is go for a walk with a horse. Usually there's the least amount of stress found there, allowing the horse and me to really feel comfortable exploring together. We'll walk anywhere—in the arena, just outside the arena, in the fields, in the forests. I'll have the horse follow my lead but then also let him have free time to investigate the world on his own while I watch over him.

At some time during this process I will get a sense of how comfortable we are with each other. In a safe area where we are both relaxed, I may stand by the horse's shoulder and place my body close to his, as if I'm trying to join with it, and I just let him feel me breathe. I slowly and softly move my hands over the horse, all while staying very grounded in my body, all while breathing deeply in through my nose and out through my mouth. As I progress around the horse like this, I sometimes move in a dancing motion, creating a rhythm that speaks to the horse, drawing him into the moment. I lean on the horse, and when there is a mounting block nearby, I walk up and spend time there as well, lying over the horse's back, breathing deeply, continuing to move my hands rhythmically all over him.

If I'm moving too fast the horse's eyes will widen, his head will rise, his jaw will tighten, his back will hollow, and he will possibly try to move away. If I have his attention, if he is relaxed, if he is in the moment with me, then he will softly blink his eyes, lower his head, loosen his jaw, relax his topline, slow his breathing, maybe lick and chew, and maybe even repeatedly yawn or slowly lower and shake his head or even his whole body. This is the great waterfall of relaxation for a horse.

I move over the horse's whole form, connecting my breathing to his, making sure he is comfortable with me everywhere, and eventually end up sitting on his back, breathing, talking to him, rubbing his neck and sides. I am relaxing him into my body, bit by bit, and I am breaking down the process as well, piece by piece, of getting on the horse's back. Trust comes from breaking things down to steps that begin slowly and build on previous progress.

Most horses are not at peace with a human on their backs. They may let themselves be ridden and may even do okay for a while, but deep down they are stressed and worried about being ridden. This usually comes from the initial saddle-training process being rushed. And most humans are not at peace on a horse's back, either. They rush themselves just as much and try to push beyond or ignore their lack of complete trust in what they are doing. Riding becomes so much the focus that we skip all the things that help being on horseback to be the experience we are hoping for.

Horses are scared of what we are capable of doing. We are scared of what horses are capable of doing. By inspiring a common curiosity for what is ahead while creating a space of safety between us, we relax with each other and form a base of peace in each other's presence. This is so important.

It's like joining the horse and yourself together and to the path you are on. Making friends with new places and new views. And once there, you'll have the feeling of not just the horse carrying you, but they will have the feeling of you carrying them as well.

I left Santa Fe and crossed the border into Arizona. I was in a world of desert and rock and the scattered people who lived among it. A dry and arid land where clouds of dust floated along the landscape, blanketing everything in their path. Arizona's beauty was raw and intense. A hot, untamed world that didn't care what I thought about it.

I took up a spot in a remote campground close to Monument Valley. As I sat beside the fire I could look out in all directions and see scattered twinkling lights from stars or houses or cars on faraway roads.

After a couple nights at the Grand Canyon, I left for California, heading toward Los Angeles. First I saw houses. Then housing developments and suburbs. Businesses and factories…overpasses and billboards. Concrete started to grow around me, and trash blew under the streaming traffic like modern-day tumbleweed. And then it happened.

A complete grayness came over the sky.

Not clouds, not rain…this was not weather. There was nothing natural about it. A muted canopy of gray hung over this world. The sun was visible only as a soft patch of yellow haze. I had heard about this. This was this world's sky.

Without much warning I had become entrenched in a steady stream of traffic that surrounded me. Buildings flew by…more gray…until all green melted away and concrete barriers appeared on both sides. The traffic thickened and picked up speed, tightening up around me, funneling me farther. I must have driven an hour in these conditions when a sign told me Los Angeles was still twenty miles away.

I stopped at a hotel right off Hollywood Boulevard. The night was cool. The streets were loud. There were lights everywhere. Not just lights but flashing, zigzagging, enticing lights.

What was I doing here?

During the first few days I attacked Hollywood with a hard-edged focus. The clock was ticking on the money I had, so I was on the computer every morning looking for jobs and apartments. My lunches consisted of dollar burritos I bought at a gas station where I had to speak to the cashier through a microphone because he was sitting behind bulletproof glass. I met with a lot of landlords, but everything was too expensive or too rundown. And all the while the gray ceiling hovered over me, the sun dulled so much I could easily stare at it.

I hit the Sunset Strip with a folder full of copies of my bartending resume. In one bar the owner laughed before he even looked at it. "Ha-ha-ha. I can't remember the last time I looked at a resume when hiring somebody. Ha-ha-ha." At another a guy with an Australian accent looked at me for approximately one second and said, "Sahrry, mate. Kids come to wurk here and they eithah becum movie stahhs or die here servin' dranks."

Days went by. All the jobs were executives, assistants, marketers, callers, and blah-blah-blah. There was something bigger than all this I told myself, and this was the work and the sacrifice, the patience and consistency to get to it. I had turned to credit cards to finance this "work and sacrifice" though. It loomed over me like the gray sky.

One night I was lying in bed, staring up at the blank hotel ceiling, and I came to a realization.

I don't like this place. And I have no idea why I am here.

I couldn't sleep. Just staring at the ceiling. For the first time in my life I realized what it meant when you can't rest right now, you need to get up and take care of something.

So I got up and turned on my computer and once again began a search to find horses.

There were barns in the San Fernando Valley. Some in Beverly Hills, of course. And then the L.A. Equestrian Center. But there was one in Hollywood called The Sunset Ranch. Twenty minutes away from me, and in their listing it said they did trail rides. Trail rides, in *Hollywood*?

When I called a girl named Lucy answered the phone. She sounded young and relaxed. "Yeah, man, come on up," she said. "You sound like just the type of person we like to have here."

The Sunset Ranch was located in the Hollywood Hills right near the famous Hollywood sign. As I drove through the entrance I could have been driving up to a ranch in Texas. Surrounded by wild sage, oak trees and hills, the ranch was at the base of Griffith Park, one of the nation's largest municipal parks with over four thousand acres and fifty-three miles of trails over untamed land.

Horses. Around seventy-five of them milled around in one main pen. All colors and sizes. They all wore halters and about half of them wore saddles.

I parked the Grand Prix and got out. A man walked by me and nodded in my direction. "Howdy," he said. He was wearing dirty, *designer* jeans and boots, with a plaid button-up shirt, sunglasses, and a straw cowboy hat. He was my age. The shirt was a little too tight for him. But it was the kind of "a little too tight" that was on purpose.

Lucy was in her mid-twenties as well. She was dressed in form-fitting jeans, a long-sleeve, Western-style, plaid shirt that was cut so that it showed off an inch of her midriff, and a similar straw cowboy hat. There was a theme here.

Lucy showed me around the ranch. It had a definitive Western feel to it. I was amazed this place could be here, twenty minutes from Hollywood Boulevard. They offered boarding and lessons but most of the ranch's income came from guided trail rides through the park.

Lucy introduced me to some of the wranglers. Most of them were young and from out of town. They had grown up with horses back home in Iowa or Montana and had come to Hollywood to try and make it in the movie industry. We then went out into the herd to bring some horses in, and pretty soon I was helping the wranglers saddle them up. A woman walked out of the main house and toward us. She looked to be in her thirties. Long brown hair fell down over her shoulders. Tight jeans, a white t-shirt, and high-heeled boots. And sunglasses, seventies style, kinda big. As she walked it seemed as if it was in slow motion, with her hair blowing in the wind. I was waiting for her theme music to come on.

"This is Audrey, the ranch manager." Lucy introduced us.

We talked a bit and Audrey seemed really happy to have me at the ranch, which was cool to hear. I didn't know if there was going to be a place for me because of my lack of experience.

"Well, if you're looking for work we have it," Audrey started. "We're going into our busy season and we need help. Why don't you go out with Dan and

Kayla today and then later this week you can go out on a night ride."

Dan and Kayla were taking out a ride of twenty people. Just like most of the other wranglers I'd met, they were in their mid-twenties. Kayla had been around the ranch for a while, so was the seasoned veteran. Dan was somewhat new.

The wranglers knew the job well, but the horses were masters at it. They tied well, bridled well, and stood patiently in line to be mounted. Once the rider was on, the horse would walk out into the main waiting area and stand there patiently. Most of the guests had never been on horses before and just let the horses move as they wanted, but the horses never took advantage of that.

I was hesitant at first. I didn't want to get in the way. But after a while I started to help with what I could and soon was getting horses from the corral and bridling them. When the ride was ready to go, I asked Kayla what horse I should ride. She looked over her shoulder and gestured toward the fence where there was one lone horse left tied.

"Greystone," she said.

He was not a horse that would catch the eye. A gray Quarter Horse gelding, standing there half asleep. I walked over and quickly tightened the girth and adjusted the stirrups. I was rushing. I didn't want to hold things up. I stopped for a second and looked into Greystone's eyes. I wanted to kind of meet him, to introduce myself in some way. I didn't know how though. He didn't seem to care, like he wasn't expecting too much.

"Come on, let's get them moving," Kayla ordered.

We rode high up into the hills and within minutes the views were spectacular. You could see all of downtown Los Angeles. Kayla was leading while Dan gave me direction on how to work the ride. We rode up and down the line of riders, keeping the people together and at the same speed while answering questions.

For a second I thought about what I was doing. *How did I end up here, in*

Hollywood, doing this? Then a rider asked me a question about her horse. I answered it. She thanked me and we moved on.

The horses all calmly walked together along the trail and not one took a bad step. The people in the saddles didn't have to do any riding. Some of them were trying to feel like they were controlling their horse, some of them might as well have just dropped the reins. It was an amusement park ride.

We came around a bend and I stopped Greystone. I saw something I had not seen for a long time.

"What's going on, man?" asked Dan as he rode by.

"Blue sky," I said.

We had ridden high enough into the hills that we were out of the suffocating smog. Below was Los Angeles, and you could actually see the city, the layer of smog over it, and the blue sky above it.

Kayla rode back to where we were. "Did we lose someone?" she said quietly. "We're supposed to have twenty. I count only nineteen."

"What? No, none of our guests have gone anywhere," said Dan.

Then a woman spoke up. "At the beginning Jules was with us, but I heard her say she was thinking about stopping. I haven't seen her since."

Kayla and Dan looked at each other.

"I can go back," I offered.

Kayla stared at me as if sizing me up right to my face. "Okay. Go. Catch up with us when you find out."

I turned Greystone around and started heading back home. We were about two miles away I figured. As we started walking back Greystone came alive and hard to control. *This is not how it's supposed to go,* he was saying. His job was to stay with the ride, stay with the herd. Taking him out of the line was foreign to him. With a little coaxing I got him going. I took him up to a trot and then a canter.

Greystone and I came around a turn and the Hollywood sign was on one side of us and downtown L.A. on the other. The horse picked up speed. His back legs pushed and his back rose and his neck arched. Faster and faster. The roar of the passing air in my ears got louder, my eyes watering.

And then we came to something I didn't expect—a fork in the path. I hadn't remembered any turns. The two paths were very close to each other and at an angle so that when coming from the other way it would have been easy to not notice the other path that joined the one we were on.

I slowed Greystone to a stop. The horse danced in place, eager to move onward. I had no idea which way to go. Greystone kept pulling forward, but I kept holding him back. And then I thought for a moment. *He knows where he is…*

I stopped holding Greystone back and let him pick the path. His choice was decisive—we were going left.

We cantered into the ranch. I looked around and spotted a woman sitting on a bench, talking on a cell phone. Greystone and I trotted over to her.

"Are you Jules?" I asked.

"Yes, I am. I decided not to go on the ride. I got down and put my horse back in the pen. Is that alright?"

With the mystery solved Greystone and I were off, back up the trail. His canter was smooth and fluid, and it felt good. I asked for more. He sped up. His head extended a bit. His mane started to blow back in the wind, the sounds of his hooves hitting the dirt quickened. Without thinking I leaned forward over his withers. I could feel it. I could feel it was okay. The surroundings started to blur...

This was galloping.

Around turns…up and down hills…running and riding in-sync. At first it was the shear exhilaration of moving with a thousand-pound animal like this, the muscle working under me, the speed. But as I settled into it I felt more of Greystone's thinking, what he was doing for me here. Letting me borrow his strength.

"This is good, we're good," I softly said to him.

Later that afternoon when we got back to the ranch, I took a moment with Greystone before I put him back with the other horses. "Thank you," I said as I spoke close to his ear and rubbed him on his neck. I had felt so much heart out there on the trail.

The ranch was run like a fine-tuned machine, processing people in and out. Guests arrived, paid, were placed on a horse, followed a guide, came back, hopefully tipped the guide, said goodbye to their horses, and left. All in about two hours. As late afternoon came it was time to prepare for the night rides, what the Sunset Ranch was famous for. Guests got there around five in the evening and enjoyed a long ride through the Hollywood Hills, down into the San Fernando Valley, stopping at a restaurant. They tied the horses outside while they had dinner and then rode back to the ranch under moonlight. On a weekend night the ranch sometimes needed every horse available to go out on the night rides. They would usually be split into two groups with three wranglers for each.

We got the horses ready. There was a system to how the horses were prepared. Two wranglers went into the pen to get the horses that were already saddled and brought them out and tied them to a long rail. Another two wranglers then tightened their girths and bridled them, and then passed them off to another wrangler who moved them down a chute to where a line of guests stood on a walkway running parallel to the chute. That wrangler then helped each guest get on a horse and gave a ten-second lesson on how to ride: "Squeeze your legs to go, pull one rein to turn, pull two reins to stop." The guest was then sent off to the main waiting area where another two wranglers fixed the stirrup length. It was a mass-production assembly line. When the dust cleared and the last rider was gone down the trail, just Lucy, Audrey, and I were left standing there.

"You did great today," Audrey said. "You're a nice rider."

"Thank you," I said humbly.

"So when can you come back? We'll get you trained on a night ride and then you'll be good to go."

"I can be here tomorrow."

The next afternoon I was on a Mustang named Scout, ready to go on my first night ride. Sonia and Nathan were the two guides leading the ride. We started up the trail with thirty riders to look after. Nathan worked with me on how to keep it organized. We moved up and down the line, slowing some people down, speeding others up.

We rode high into the hills with great views in all directions and then down into San Fernando Valley, traversing steep slopes where riders had to go one-by-one. As we descended, we crossed a beautiful field to a wooded path that opened up into a suburban area and took two tunnels under roadways. We then crossed a cable bridge (with a little bit of a not-so-fun sway to it) where it was very important to not let more than three horses on the bridge at the same time. We came around a corner and rode right into the backyard of a restaurant with hitching posts outside.

We had the riders dismount in an orderly fashion and tied each horse to the rail with the rope halter/lead line they wore under their bridles. As the guests went inside to eat and drink for an hour, we went through all the horses, loosened girths, and took bridles off and draped them around the saddle horns.

Around nine o'clock the guests meandered out and one-by-one we got them back on their horses. Off into the night we rode. The Southern California sky was so clear it allowed the moon to light our way like some sort of sun from another world. The return ride was much harder. Not just because it was dark but because the horses knew they were headed home. They picked up trots and even canters and got a little out of control. It was like trying to hold back a stampede. The guests had a few margaritas in them, so they were also a little out of control.

The night ride was work, looking after thirty people on thirty horses. It was hard physically and mentally. But I loved it. And once again I was in a different world, away from everything, while I was doing it. I was working the rear of the ride, the last rider, and as the ranch came into view, I stopped Scout for a moment to watch those in front of me walk down the path. Perfect silhouettes of horses and riders in the bright moonlight. A wonderful sense of calm came over me.

"These are the moments, Scout," I said aloud. "We work the whole ride to get to little moments like this."

Scout kept trying to move forward and I kept holding him back. His eye shifted back to me. *What are we doing? I want to go home. I get to go home now.* All he wanted was to go home. He too should get his moment—getting home and taking the saddle off. So on to the ranch we went.

I thought about that. The moment didn't feel right if the horse wasn't enjoying it, too, in some way. I had to make the horse stand there so I could feel something good, when all the while the horse wasn't feeling something good.

I wondered what a horse *could* feel. If he was capable of feeling what I was feeling when I stopped to watch the riders in the moonlight.

We got the riders off safely and put the horses back in the corral.

"Great job," Sonia said to me. "You were great with the horses and great with the people. You really looked after the ride well."

As I walked back to the Grand Prix, I felt something.

I can do this.

7 | Blood Paid

HORSE BREAKING. Colt starting. Starting the horse. In the past it has been called many things. It can be done many ways. A thousand different horses, a thousand different first rides. It can be daunting and scary. Or it can be relaxed and full of confidence. It is what we make of it. It is exactly whatever *we* want it to be. We are the guide. We have chosen to sit on the horse's back and ask him to move. And he will react and respond only in ways he has learned, and we can then choose how we will respond.

If we have taken care of our relationship with our horse, then we have built a foundation from which all else will grow. Who we've seen the horse to be in the groundwork will be the horse we will see in the riding. So we can work on that first ride from the ground for as long as we need. Days, weeks, months, years. The road gets easier, not harder. That first ride gets taken care of before you even get on the horse. Then, we can think of riding very simply: We are just leading the horse around, something we have done many times, but we are now just doing it from the horse's back.

First rides should be kind of blurry in their remembrance. They should happen in small bits, short little rides that don't last too long, just a few steps here and there while bareback maybe. Solid experiences that let the horse learn the balance to carry us, how to see and feel and hear us "up there." But this is for the human as much as for the horse. We need time, as well, to get acquainted and comfortable with the physicality of the horse and how he feels and moves under us. The old saying *slow is fast and fast is slow* is an old saying for a reason. Many years down the road we should look back and remember the time, the feeling, but maybe not the exact first ride, all because it was just a spontaneous moment one day where everything felt right, and it was as if the horse asked us to come up, with the moment being no more or less beautiful than all the other beautiful moments leading up to it.

We've developed a feeling with the horse from all our time and groundwork together. It's in our gut now. Trust it. We can tell when something is going well and when it needs a little help. The horse is in this with us. Feel his energy, watch his body language and what he has to say. There will be times where we will sense he is confused, worried, or frustrated. But because we have already worked with his thoughts and feelings on the ground, it has prepared him well and he has learned to think and process, to have patience and to problem-solve, and to look to us for help. There may also be times where we sense he is not trying his hardest. We have to inspire him, just as we would on the ground, or he will realize we are not as confident when on him and he may learn to take advantage of that.

Above all, the horse is our friend, and our friend is carrying us on his back. We have to be respectful and grateful for this and realize he needs our help along the way. On the ground he can see us; it's so much easier for him to follow us. Now he can only see our knees and toes in his peripheral vision. It has become a completely physical feeling for him. The physical difference between being on the ground and riding can be drastic. But the mental, spiritual, and actual feeling can be one and the same. Down the road and out into the world there will be tough times, challenges that find us, but if we have prepared our horse, facing these will only serve to bring us closer.

At the heart of it is the beautiful feeling of moving together, I need the horse and the horse needs me. And when horse and rider move in unison in mind, body, and soul...we are both carried to a place higher than who we are without each other.

I was working as a wrangler at the Sunset Ranch. Western saddles, Quarter Horses, cowboy hats, and dust. For the most part in the beginning, I was just trying to fit in and do the best job I could with what I knew how to do. I was taking in an immense amount of knowledge daily. It was not only a different style of riding at this ranch, it was a different style of horsemanship.

But I felt like I had been doing the job for years, working with the people and the horses. There was something about it I knew right off, that I fit in with. Leading these rides, you had to be definitive in your directions for human and horse, yet completely laid back, calm, and relaxed for human and horse. I felt very comfortable looking after the horses and being *aware* of what was going on. There was something I could see when a human and a horse were together, something I could help with if they were having trouble.

I found an unfurnished apartment in a cool little Hollywood neighborhood. I made a comfy bed out of blankets, towels, sweatshirts, and sweaters. It worked well and I got good sleep. My suitcase doubled as a table and I set my laptop on it. That was pretty much it. I didn't spend much time there. I was always at the ranch. I abandoned all thought of the scripts I had written.

There were horses.

Once again immersing myself in horses had done its job. All thoughts of Ally—and Karen—ceased. I moved into another new world, letting myself be taken far away.

The night rides were the main draw. They were incredible. I ended up working with everyone at the ranch but gravitated toward Sonia and Dan. When Sonia and I took a ride out it always went well. We were very similar in how we liked the rides to go. Dan and I hit it off because we were the same age and had the same sense of humor. We had a good time when we rode together.

I would sometimes work the day shift, eat a quick lunch, and then work the night ride. Sometimes there were three or four private rides going out in one night and wranglers would have to lead each ride of eight to twelve people on their own. These were the most stressful. You had to lead the ride, move up and down the line to help people, and ride to the rear of the line now and then to get the slower horses going, all on your own.

I started working every day. I couldn't get enough. The tips weren't great, but it was enough to pay rent and buy food. I started to gravitate toward certain horses. Scout the Mustang, and Gus, a sorrel Quarter Horse. The more rides I had with them the more a working relationship developed between us. It was a job though, and it was work. My focus was on the rides going well. I didn't really think much about the horses as individuals and how they felt about it. I was loving the job too much.

On my days off I went to the Hollywood Library and systematically took out every book they had on horses. I bought notebooks and filled them with thoughts and notes on what I was reading. I decided I should buy my first horse book: *The Complete Equine Veterinary Manual* by Tony and Marcy Pavord. I read it and made notecards that on one side had symptoms of a horse injury, disease, or sickness and then on the other side had the name of the injury, disease, or sickness along with the standard protocol of how to help the horse. While I was stuck in Los Angeles traffic, I would pull out the notecards and quiz myself. *Azoturia, colic, navicular, strangles, laminitis, proud flesh, hematomas…*

One day at the ranch Nathan was getting ready to ride a new horse. The horse was unsettled from the start, pulling back with head high and eyes wide, hindquarters dancing back and forth like windshield wipers. *Why get on?* I thought. The ride seemed destined for failure. The horse was going to keep doing what he was doing except Nathan would be on his back while he was doing it. I thought there must be something that could be done to help the horse, to set the ride up for success before someone got on.

But Nathan got on. Maybe it was the fact there were people watching. Maybe Nathan did not want to feel like he was fearful of riding the horse. Maybe he just wanted to show the horse he could win.

His ride lasted five seconds. The horse bucked, throwing Nathan forward onto the horse's neck. Then the horse reared sky high. Nathan fell backward, pulling on the reins as he went, as well as the horse's head. This brought the whole horse toppling over on top of him.

There was a gasp from those watching. In a cloud of dust Nathan and the horse hit the ground on their backs. The horse just narrowly missed landing on Nathan. They both got up.

"That's enough," said Audrey. "That horse can't be used here."

Wow, crazy horse, I thought. As they both got up from the ground and Nathan passed the horse off to another wrangler, I looked into the horse's eyes and my thought instantly changed. What I saw...the horse needed help. The horse was frantic and lost and needed help in some way. The horse didn't know what was going on. The horse had no sense of what to do. A bad past experience? The saddle hurting? Whatever it was I saw in those eyes, it was *real*. It was a real feeling, and it frustrated me that I couldn't figure it out.

The next day the horse wasn't at the ranch when I got there.

I didn't hear where he went.

———————

"You do a great job here. The horses and the people really like you," Audrey said to me.

"Thanks, that's real great to hear. It's fun work."

"So…how would you feel about giving some riding lessons?"

I was taken aback. There were people on the ranch who had been there five years longer than me. "Ahh, really?" I replied.

"Yeah. Sonia is our only instructor and her lesson schedule is full. Would you like to do it?"

"Well…thank you for asking me," I said, still stunned. "Umm…well are you sure I am the most qualified? Some of the other wranglers here are great and they have much more experience than me. I don't know if I would feel comfortable."

"You're great," Audrey said with a smile and her head tilted to one side, like I was a little kid she needed to make feel good. "You have a way with the horses, in how you work with them, in how you ride, and you're so good with the people and…not everybody else is, you know what I mean?" She was still smiling.

I stood and thought about it for a second. I didn't want to give lessons just because I was asked. I wanted to feel like I had something to offer.

I thought about it for a second longer.

I could feel it.

"I'll do it."

I think I put more into those first lessons than any riding instructor in history. I wrote notes and ideas out the week before and had the whole lesson planned. I wanted the students I was teaching to not just learn how to ride a horse, I wanted them to get to *know* horses. I had them work with the horses on the ground first to get comfortable with them, to learn how they moved, how they communicated…and how they *thought*. I wanted my students to get a *feel* for horses and to feel safe with them at all times.

So I always started my lessons on the ground with leading and lunge-ing, grooming and tacking up, then my students would ride. The whole time I talked about horse care, anatomy, history. I laid out everything I knew for the student. And when the lesson was finished, one hour had sometimes stretched to two. The students seemed very happy and kept coming back. I was having a blast.

Then one day Audrey came up to me.

"Listen," she started. "Your lessons seem to be going great and that's so awesome. But you can't go over the one-hour time limit."

"Oh, I'm sorry. It's just to have time to do the groundwork and then ride it sometimes takes longer than the hour."

"You shouldn't worry about doing stuff on the ground. Just have them ride. That's all they want anyway. Okay?"

"Ahh, alright. Sure," I said.

It didn't feel right to me, but I did what Audrey told me to do. And after a few weeks, a great thing happened. My students *asked* to pay for longer lessons because they *wanted* to do the groundwork. My heart was in it and that was infectious. I loved seeing what could happen when a horse and a human really understood each other and connected. I felt I was actually seeing my students change for the better, and I hoped it would stay with them when they went back to their lives outside of horses.

Ideas were developing in my head. I felt ready to explore my own ways of working with horses.

"I wanted to ask you, Audrey," I started. "Would you mind if in my spare time I worked with some of the horses? You know, maybe tried to get them to be better with some of the things they do around the ranch?"

"Go for it," she said, shrugging her shoulders like it didn't matter. "Have fun."

That was all I needed to hear.

Approaching horses. Many of the horses at the ranch were hard to catch. I worked on my body language, learning how to approach and retreat to get a horse comfortable with me walking up to him. I felt an amazing sense of fulfillment when I could eventually walk up to a horse that would usually run away from humans.

Round penning and "hooking on." I was fascinated by this. The idea of working with a horse free, with no halter or lead line, in a circular paddock had been popularized by the "natural horsemanship" movement. "Hooking on," where the horse would choose to follow me around wherever I went, was a central tenet of this movement. I found if I had this with a horse, other training went much easier. The horse had chosen to work with me while he was free. It was a major point in our relationship.

My riding seat. People weren't afraid of riding horses, they were afraid of falling off horses. I thought if I had the best riding seat ever then I would be relaxed and freed up to think about other things while in the saddle.

Cantering. It was the godly movement. And there was a feel to it. It was all in the hips and pelvic bone and breathing.

Working with as many horses as I could. I realized that the more horses I handled, the better my knowledge and feel for all horses would get. Gus, Scout, Brad, Chief, Sundance, Mouse, Lona, Smokey. Sometimes I would just go in and hang out in the main corral with all seventy-five horses and soak up the interaction.

I had a ranch full of horses and the freedom to dive into it any way I wanted. I had no past in this land. I was filled up every day and leaving happy. The sleep I got on my makeshift bed on the floor was some of the best I'd ever had.

I spent most of my days and nights in the saddle. I continued giving lessons, and I was training horses any time I could. I started to develop a system of my own and a reputation as the guy who could ride any horse. And one day while I was working with a horse in the arena, I felt it.

No one on the ranch thought it could be done. *But I can do it. I can feel it.*

I decided to train Smokey to tie.

Smokey was a gray Quarter Horse. He always had a sour look on his face like he was bothered by something. He was good enough on the trail—no one ever looked to ride him though. What distinguished him the most was one simple thing: Smokey didn't tie. No one *ever* tried to tie him. If you had him in a halter and lead rope and approached a tie rail, he would violently throw himself back, rearing and pulling with all his might.

I started slow.

As usual, the moment he saw me approach the rail, his eyes shot wide open and his body pulled back. I stayed quiet and patient and moved with him, not fighting him in any way. When he fought, I relaxed. My eyes were soft, my breathing loose. Again and again he pulled back, but I just moved with him, and when he settled we would approach the rail again. Eventually I was able to walk to the rail and lay the rope over it while he danced in place without pulling back. He quieted more, but his head was still in the air with eyes wide. I walked him away from the rail, and he immediately released all his tension: lowering his head, blinking, and licking and chewing—signs of relaxed thinking rather than fear. I helped him to see that pulling back got him nowhere, but relaxing while the lead line was gently laid over the rail got him what he wanted—away from the rail. I hoped eventually enough positive experiences would help him gain confidence and trust me when I went to really tie him.

I next looped the rope around the rail and used the rail as leverage. When Smokey pulled back I just let some slack out so he could move and wouldn't have pressure to fight against, then slowly took back on the line to reel him back in. He had the feeling of being tied, without really being tied. When he stood for a while and relaxed without pulling back, I simulated "untying" the rope, and we would go do something else, away from the rail, something he thought was easy.

For three days we practiced this and when it came time to try tying him…
Success!

I had spent so much time laying the rope over the rail, pretending to tie it, tugging on the line, trying to show him it was alright, that when I finally tied him, he stood there perfectly. I went really slowly, watched him the whole time, and untied him after only a minute and walked him away. I repeated again and again. He was great.

It went well, but my knowledge and experience were limited. Even worse, I didn't know they were limited. I was riding a wave of confidence in my feel for horses. And I started to get cocky.

The following Tuesday I went up to the ranch. As I usually did first thing in the morning, I went to see my horses—Gus and Scout. And Smokey. I decided to bring Smokey out to work for the day and have him go on some rides. I wanted to show the people at the ranch that Smokey was a good horse and that he could learn. And I wanted to find a moment where I could show them what I had taught him.

I wanted to show off.

Smoke was pretty dirty, so I took him to the wash area to hose him down. He had done well with our lessons. His confidence was growing through me, as was mine through him. Trust was forming.

I had never practiced tying him in the wash area. But what if I was able to tie him there, hose him down, and everybody saw it?

The gray horse hesitated when I brought him near the rail. I expected that. I got him close and then stood with him for a while and let him relax. I then took his lead rope and draped it over the rail, moving slowly. As usual he tensed up, but he stood with me. After a bit, I went to tie the rope. Smokey backed up a few steps, and the line tightened in my hands. I talked to him and he relaxed.

He could tie and I wanted everybody to see it.

I began tying the quick-release knot, keeping an eye on Smokey. I always watched him, looking for the first clue of his tension erupting into violence. I moved slowly. All was going well as I looped the rope...slowly...

slowly…. And then I took my eye off the horse for one little moment…

In a blur the lead line snapped tight and broke as Smokey threw himself back with all his might. A millisecond and it was done. The gelding stood there calmly, looking at me, a broken lead line dangling from his head.

My left hand was throbbing. I looked down.

My index finger was half gone. A porcelain-like white bone protruded from the torn flesh. A thick, steady gush of blood was erupting from the half finger, swirling around my hand like the red stripe on a candy cane. It streamed to the ground and formed a neat little puddle in the dirt.

My first thought: *Oh no, I won't get to be with the horses for a while.*

My second thought: *Stop the bleeding, find the missing piece.*

I quickly took off the button-up shirt I was wearing and wrapped it around my wounded hand. Then I scanned the area around my feet. I was calm, all business. There was a massive throbbing but no pain. I grabbed Smokey's dangling lead with my good hand, afraid he would step on what I was looking for.

Minutes went by and I started to get nervous. If I wanted any chance of reattaching my finger, I needed to get to a hospital as soon as possible. Finally, about fifteen feet away from the rail, I found it.

It must have shot off like a cork.

It's something, picking up a piece of your own body. The fingertip looked fake, like a prop from a cheesy eighties horror movie.

I quickly returned Smokey to the main pen, then stopped by my car and grabbed the small cooler that held my lunch. I dumped the food on the ground as I walked quickly toward the office, leaving the ice packs in place.

"Kayla, I've hurt my hand, and I need someone to drive me to the hospital," I announced as I stepped through the door.

"Oh my God, oh my God, oh my God!" Kayla stood up from behind the desk and started moving frantically around, eyes fixated on the bloody shirt wrapped around my left hand.

"Kayla…" I said calmly. "Kayla, listen. I'm okay. I just need somebody to drive me to the nearest hospital."

An empty Styrofoam cup sat on the desk. *Perfect.* I grabbed it and walked outside the office to where the hose was neatly coiled beside the building. I washed the piece of finger off and put it in the cup, then placed the cup on the ice packs in my cooler.

Within half an hour I was at the hospital. I had cleaned and transported my severed finger correctly, but unfortunately, it had fallen into a high-bacteria area—horse pasture. There was no way the doctors would take the risk of reattaching it.

After two hours of surgery, I walked out of the hospital with my hand wrapped in a ball of bandages. I got a cab back to my apartment, walked in, and sat down.

Did that really just happen?

What had I done?

It was just me, a lonely apartment, a bandaged hand, and the pain.

It was mind-piercing pain. I couldn't think. My body was in a constant cringe. The only thing that even remotely helped was keeping my arm raised. So I made a little "prop station" out of some books and clothes beside my bed, and I lied down with my hand propped straight up.

I realized how alone I was. I had gotten over-confident and made a stupid mistake and now I was a guy in a small, empty apartment in a city I didn't like with no horses…and short half a finger. Without the horses I had nothing in this land. My one thing, my one good thing, had been taken away from me. And it was my fault.

I had gotten in over my head.

8 | Rise Again Better

I ONCE SAW a young boy who was scared. He got something in his eye and it hurt and he didn't know what to do.

He started to cry and jump around frantically. His parents tried to explain it was no big deal and he should come to them so they could get it out. The boy kept crying and jumping around. The parents became frustrated. They yelled at him and grabbed him and held him still and didn't let him rub his eyes while they told him he was wrong for not listening. At that moment it wasn't about helping the child anymore.

The boy was in pain and scared. A combination that gets in the way of calm, logical thinking. The child was not able to think about what was best to do in that situation.

Horses are like this, as adult humans are too, sometimes. Hopefully horses and humans have friends who can help them by providing the calm and logical thinking they lack when scared and in pain. And hopefully, eventually, horses and humans can provide it for themselves.

We might not have chosen to be with horses to have a responsibility like this, but that is exactly what we have—a responsibility to look out for them no matter what they are going through and no matter how much it does or doesn't make sense to us. There *will* be tough times when horses need our help to safely guide them, whether it is a moment of panic or a moment of frustration. We must do our best to understand this, work on how we can help them, and be patient. If we make peace with the fact that all relationships have challenges and clashes, we then free ourselves up to work on the ways to get through it.

Every horse is different. A less confident horse will need us to guide his movement in stressful situations. That's the unforeseen, anxious jigs or jumps we need to know how to move with, both on the ground and in the saddle. A more confident horse may test us to see if we are a good leader while directing him as a rider. That's the kicking out or the bucking we need to know how to absorb or counter. A horse in pain may spook, bolt, or rear. That's the reaction caused by a saddle that doesn't fit properly, a chiropractic issue, Lyme disease, or one of many other conditions. The journey of being with your horse through these challenges—and understanding his behavior and deciphering symptoms, then applying a course of action—is one of utmost honor.

We can never say it is going to be easy. But we can always say it will be worth it.

Experience in this gives us confidence. Hardships teach us. The challenging times are here to help us. They are here to right the ship in some way. This is sometimes hard to believe, especially when an event is particularly devastating, especially when it's not turning out the way we hoped. There is something in the fear, something in the heartbreak, something in the pain that is only available there, even though the gifts of the experience are sometimes not quite comprehensible at the moment.

The goal isn't to not be scared at all, it is to be smart. Nobody makes up being scared—it is our inner voice telling us to look out, and we should listen to that voice; it is there to help us. But if I told you that you would never fall off a horse, your inner voice would be calmer and more confident. So that tells me we need to have a mind that is relaxed and steady, and a body that sits the horse deeply and naturally.

We need to be grounded. We need to have good, strong roots.

A "natural seat" is when we are perfectly balanced with the horse while riding him. Our relaxed body follows and fits in with the horse's movement. Our eyes are soft, confident, and looking where we want to be; our back is relaxed and straight with a vertical line that follows from our ear, to our shoulder, to our hip; our hands hold the reins with a soft feel; our thighs are free and easy, our pelvic bone effortlessly moves with the motion of the horse. And it's all tied together by our breathing, long and deep, and our mind, calm and focused. Grounded, with good, strong roots.

There are times when the ride will get rough or when we will see a bumpy road ahead. It's bound to happen. That's riding. That's life. Our mind has to get a little more focused. Our body has to get a little more grounded. And our natural seat has to get a little deeper.

When we fall off a horse, almost every time, it is over the shoulder of the horse or off his side. It is very hard to recover our balance when movement thrusts us too far forward or sideways while on the horse's back. Also, when we are scared, our body tenses up and goes into the fetal position. It's an instinctive human reaction designed to protect our most precious things—our head and neck. But this also pushes our balance forward and in a much more precarious position. It all comes down to one thing—the more forward or to the side and out of our seat we get, the more chance we fall.

Think of the most extreme sport in the world where people have to stay on a horse: bronco riding. Watch how far back riders lean to sit the bucks. Watch John Wayne ride in a few of his movies. You'll notice that as he got older he leaned more and more back in the saddle to make up for the riding ability he lost. When riding gets tough our shoulders should lean back and our feet should shift forward. It's not about looking pretty anymore, it's about staying on. This proactively balances us, and grounds and roots us to the horse. And then we need to breathe. And breathe more deeply. And keep breathing.

Then we need to think about how we guide the horse in his movement.

In the case of a scared horse, for example, he wants to *go-run-get-away*, and when we get scared while riding, we want to *whoa-stand-stop*. Two conflicting ideas. What we need to do is meet the horse halfway: He needs to move to feel relaxed, we need to have control to feel relaxed. So let the horse move and just *control* how he moves.

I sometimes use a figure-eight pattern. The figure eight is like a track that keeps me and the horse in a quiet place, turning in two circles, with a constant change of direction in the middle to hold our attention. We meet each other halfway. I guide the horse while letting him feel free to move.

If the horse surprises me with erratic movement, I guide him into a circle. The faster we're going, the slower we do it. I get my deep seat, choke up on a rein to help the horse bend his neck, and then use my leg to "disengage" the hindquarters—not a one-rein stop, but a one-rein *slow down*.

If we are living, we are challenged by the sudden stops, starts, and movements we have to face. There *will* be spooks and bucks. But we can flow with them, learn from them, and transcend them with a quiet mind and the confidence to take the lead.

We just have to get a deep seat, keep our mind in the middle of the saddle, and ride the ride.

———————

I lay back and turned on the little TV I had hooked up, and *Rio Bravo*, a movie starring John Wayne, was on. It was John Wayne week on AMC, and I was watching them all. It became the focal point of my days. Each day I would get up and check the TV listings, and then my whole day would revolve around *The Quiet Man* playing at seven o'clock. For some reason while I was watching those John Wayne movies life wasn't so bad. And I was able to forget I hadn't left the apartment in a week.

At the hospital I watched as the layers of bandages were slowly unwrapped. I saw the bloody stump for the first time. A shudder ran through me. It couldn't have been more grotesque. It looked like it had been gnawed on by a dog.

"It will look better in time," said the doctor.

In the long days sitting around my apartment, I tried to get into my horse books, but I had lost the inspiration. I was so disappointed with myself. My mom called but I couldn't bring myself to call her back. I didn't want to tell her. And I didn't want to lie. So I avoided talking to her altogether. I talked to a few friends back home, Josh and Brendan. They told me if I wanted to come back to Maine, I could stay with them.

One day I was at the grocery store across the street. I recognized Frank Darabont, director of the movie *The Shawshank Redemption*. There he was, standing in line right in front of me, the man responsible for one of my favorite movies of all time. The man responsible for a movie that had inspired millions to *get busy living*.

I thought about what I should do with the moment. But the more I thought about it, the more I just stared at his back. I realized he was a regular person. Just like me, with hopes and dreams, failures and successes, good times and bad. I remembered something he had said in an interview once, how he thought there were probably people out there working in shoe stores or as barbers or truck drivers who were better directors than him, but the difference was he put in the time and effort and perseverance to make it happen.

I decided it was time to go back to the ranch.

"Does it hurt?" asked Lucy.

"Not really. If it does I just elevate it above my heart so the blood isn't rushing down into it."

"What's it going to look like when the bandages come off?" asked Kayla.

"Don't know yet."

"We all want to kill Smokey for what he did to you, man," said Dan with an angry look on his face.

"Nah. Wasn't his fault."

"What do you mean it wasn't his fault?" said Dan. "He's a stupid, ignorant horse. He's worthless."

I looked at Dan, studying him to see if he really meant what he was saying. I had assumed everyone thought of it like I did. It was completely my mistake. I was trying to do something Smokey wasn't ready for yet and he was just doing what made him feel safe. It was just self-preservation for Smokey. He wasn't trying to hurt anybody.

"No, guys, I made the mistake," I said. "I was over-confident and I had no business trying to tie him there. Smokey is a good guy, just scared of being tied, that's all. Someone made him that way. It's not his fault."

"Whatever," said Kayla. "I'm not ever touching him."

A very regretful feeling came over me. I had given Smokey a bad reputation.

My heart sunk.

When I walked back to the car later that day I felt something reawakening in me. It was time to stop hurting and get back to work.

At my apartment I took out a little wooden box I'd brought west. In it was an assortment of bone beads, plastic beads, sinew, and leather. I had always been interested in Native American culture and at one point taught myself how to make bone-bead jewelry. I sat down that night and set to making a bracelet. It had inch-long bone beads I let sit in coffee to give them a wooden color. It had green, silver, and black beads. All strung together by tightly wound sinew, with leather draw strings at each end.

———

I went back to the ranch the next day with my finger still bandaged and a pair of deerskin gloves to wear. I tore the left glove a little so my bandaged finger would fit.

"Are you sure you can do this?" asked Audrey.

"Yeah, I'll be fine." I started walking to the corrals.

"I like the bracelet you're wearing," she said.

"Thanks," I replied.

It wasn't a *bracelet* bracelet. It wasn't jewelry. It had a different purpose. I was going to wear it every time I was around horses. It would serve as a reminder that my safety was in my own hands. It was a *choice* to be safe. It was not up to the horse or luck. It was up to the choices I made and how I carried myself—my preparation, my knowledge, my awareness, and the positions I put myself in.

It was going to keep me honest.

And so with my new gloves and my bracelet I was back doing rides. And on every ride I thought about what I wanted to do next.

I needed help. I had the heart and the desire with the horses, but I needed someone to guide me, to watch over me. I looked into horse-training schools but didn't commit. The term *trainer* didn't feel right to me. Plus I had no money.

I was going to have to go a different route. I needed to gain experience while working.

Guest ranches.

I went to work on the internet researching guest ranches in Montana and Wyoming. Utah and Colorado. New Mexico and Arizona. For a week I looked at ranch after ranch, and when I saw one where I thought I could fit in, I called them. It was summer, though, and they were all fully staffed, and soon I was running out of numbers to call.

Then I came across the Rancho de la Osa.

It was in Sasabe, Arizona, less than a mile from the Mexican border. At over three hundred years old it was one of the oldest ranches in America.

The architecture of the ranch was classic southwestern with adobe buildings and different shades of turquoise outlining the doors and the windows.

Something about the place made my heart jump.

I was slowly learning to always notice and respect and listen to that reaction.

I called and talked with one of the owners, Monica. She got right to the point.

"Yes, we're looking for a cowboy for our upcoming season. Call back tomorrow and talk with my husband, Tom. He does all the hiring. Thanks."

Excellent. They had a position open. But she'd said "for a cowboy."

I wasn't a cowboy.

That night I was all over the Rancho de la Osa website, flipping back and forth between pages. The ranch was far from any real civilization, situated in the middle of the Sonoran Desert, the most floral desert in the world. The website showed pictures of a land dominated by thorny mesquite trees, yucca and ocotillo plants, barrel and prickly pear cactus, and of course the classic, tall saguaro cactus with its outstretched arms.

And there were horses. Lots of them.

When I called back the next day Tom picked up.

"That's all your experience?" he said surprised.

"Yes, sir," I stated. And then I said the truest words I had to give him. "But I can tell you this: you won't find anyone more honest, reliable, and hardworking than me. And Tom, you won't find anyone who loves working with horses and the people that want to connect with them more than me."

I said it strong and let it sit. I had to wait and see if he was the kind of man that could hear the truth in a voice over a phone.

His end was silent for a while. Then he spoke very directly. "On a ranch in the middle of nowhere honesty and reliability are worth quite a bit. Where are you from again?"

"Maine."

"Maine, huh? Why do you want to work way out here?"

"It's where everything is leading me right now. My passion is with the horses, and what I've also found is I have a passion for helping people with horses. That and I want to be somewhere where every day I wake up and I'm excited to be where I am. Do you know what I mean?"

Tom was quiet for a moment. Then, "Yeah, I do."

He told me he would talk it over with Monica and get back to me.

A day went by, then another. The longer without a phone call, the more it meant bad news. It made sense though. I had so much less experience than the usual people working those ranches.

But I started living as if it was happening. I started packing, getting ready. I saw it in my mind. I couldn't see myself not working there.

I was believing it to see it.

9 | Voice of the Guardian

IF ALL THINGS are constantly in motion and change is eternal, then it's important to have a feel for the motion and the change that our soul is seeking.

We have to remember we are leading our lives. We have choices, every day, every moment. And leading our lives isn't that far away from what it's like to lead a horse while riding him.

There's an age-old debate out there between fate and freedom. Is our future set, or is it made up as we go? We all seem to have a journey within us—a soul's adventure. Our unique passions, gifts, and life-callings are specific to us, and our paths surely seem to have certain pre-ordained meetings and coincidences. While navigating these adventures, however, it seems we are given freedom of choice. Think about it, really feel it, and ask yourself, *Do you feel forced in your choices? Like they are already made for you?*

We may have free choice, but one way always feels better than the other. It often feels there is something guiding us, something urging us to stay on some sort of course. This can give us a feeling of security—that we are not alone and that something is looking out for us. Going faster, slower, left or right, or calling it a day—there's some sort of voice inside that leads the way and it seems to know what will happen before it happens. But this voice does not make us choose. That freedom is ours.

Intuition and visualization can seem a lot like magic. They kind of are—they're invisible, come from some unknown place within, and make things happen out of nowhere. And with a horse your intuition and visualization, combined with your feel and energy, can make a walk, trot, or canter appear. The beginning of those walks, trots, and canters is always in that inner voice, the feel somewhere deep within of what's to happen next. It's the instinctual understanding of what will take us to a higher place in life. And the more we understand this voice and listen to it, the more we trust where it is taking us.

I see the horse walking while I am riding. I slowly start to move my pelvic bone in the right motion and the horse, open-hearted to my guidance, has the thought of *walking* come into his mind, and moves out in stride. I feel the trot would be nice, so I shift my pelvic bone into the one-two motion of a trot and the horse syncs this movement with mine, picking up the gait. A canter would be beautiful right now, I can *feel* us doing it, so I *think* canter and…

The horse relies on magic too. He feels my energy, sees visions in his mind, and makes his own choices. If we are fully in tune with each other, then when I provide a "feel" to the horse, his inner voice hears what I am asking and takes it from there. It's the unification that we all dream about—horse and human moving as one, as if of one mind. As if listening to one voice.

How do we get there? Never-ending practice. The whole journey of a life, with no such thing as destination or perfection.

There is always a forward path sitting there for every horse and human. First we feel it. Then we envision it. And then we have to put in the work. We can't sit there waiting for something to come. If we get up and just start, that puts life in motion. It might take a lot of work or it might not, there are no rules either way. What it does take, is us starting to *live like we are going to do it*. That's not my rule. Not the horse's either.

It's life's rule.

I couldn't recall feeling that excited about something in a long time. The kind of excited when something is on your mind constantly and you feel good constantly. I realized a feeling like that didn't just come to you, you had to make it happen.

What kind of had me nervous though was the last thing Tom had said: "Well, we're looking forward to having you. I'm sure you'll be a great cowboy."

Cowboy. I was not a cowboy. I told him I was not a cowboy. Most of the people who worked these guest ranches were known as "wranglers"; they looked after the horses and took people out on rides. I could do that. But the riders who worked at the Rancho de la Osa, apparently, were cowboys.

I drove to a Western-wear store in Burbank. I didn't have much money. I chose one pair of Wrangler jeans and then looked at the different hats. For an hour I tried on all types but nothing seemed right. Then I saw it. A chocolate-brown Stetson with a perfectly curved brim and a black band around it. It fit.

"This is the one," I said to the man helping me.

Back at the Sunset Ranch I returned to working the rides full-time, but I started to get bored with it. I loved doing it, but my mind was now on working with the horses, one on one. During any spare time I had, I was off alone with the horses while the rest of the wranglers hung out in the office.

I was working with the horses from a different mindset now. Every time I looked down at my bone-bead bracelet I thought about what I could do for them and how much easier and simpler I could make the training for them. *How I could make myself better* for them.

It was around this time Jeff came to work at the ranch. He was a medium-build man in his early fifties with a beard. He had just sold his ranch in Colorado and moved to Los Angeles to live with his son. He wore a small Stetson-like hat with a hawk feather on it, and his boots were worn and his jeans were torn. He came in with a relaxed attitude and nothing to prove. He just wanted to be around horses, and he had a way with them. He was a real cowboy, while we were all just kids who knew how to work the rides. A lot of the other wranglers were threatened by this.

I saw it as an opportunity.

"Good. No straight lines, no hard movements. And don't stare at him," Jeff said as he helped me approach Butch. The Mustang was the hardest to catch of all the horses. When they saw me trying to catch him, most of the wranglers offered help or went to get a lariat to rope him. They didn't understand it wasn't about just "catching" him. But when Jeff saw me in the paddock with Butch, he just watched and offered advice.

"Don't rush," he said. "Be confident with your body language; believe in what you're doing. Be deliberate but balanced with a nonaggressive posture. Round yourself and your movement. There… there…yeah, and now when he lets you get as close as you have ever gotten, what should you do?"

"Relax for a second, maybe turn and back off. Let that soak?"

"Yeah. He'll see the best way to make you go away is to let you approach him. That'll get him to stand for you, get him to give you a chance. You get him to just give you a chance, then you show him you ain't so bad.

"After a while it all just flows together," continued Jeff. "The horse sees you match inside and out. Your actions are as good as your intentions. And the horse lets you in."

The hazy sky had a blue coolness to it for my last ride at the Sunset Ranch. Sonia and Dan were taking out the first group of twenty-five riders. I was leading the second ride of thirty-five, along with two new wranglers, Jenny and Ellen.

Audrey came over to me while I was saddling Gus. "Did anyone tell you about Greystone?" she said. "He died."

"What?"

"Yeah," she said sadly. "I saw it happen right in front of me. He died right there in the pasture."

I tried to go back to work but I had to stop and sit on a nearby bench. Gus quietly stood over me as I held one rein. I was overwhelmed with a feeling of sadness. A sadness for how the old horse died and how I never...

I didn't thank him enough. I just...used him.

And now Greystone was just another horse that died in a pasture and was carted off or buried somewhere, unmarked. Famous racehorses had burials in fields with headstones but Greystone, a horse who gave his heart just as much, he was...

I looked down at the bone-bead bracelet. I'd started wearing it as a reminder to always *think safe, think calm, think horse.* But when I looked at it now I thought of Greystone. Then I looked up at Gus, the small, sorrel Quarter Horse standing near me.

He was still here. Gus wasn't gone yet. He was still in this world.

I stood up and slowly rested my hand on his forehead. His eyes softly closed. I laid my forehead against his and closed my eyes. "Thank you, my friend," I said. "Thank you for all you do in helping me to find my way."

The night ride started out well. I was leading and we were on time. The horses started getting "trotty," and I had to keep telling people to slow down. It was a big crew and a lot of times on the big rides you were just hoping to keep it contained rather than have everything go perfect, especially with two wranglers who were somewhat new riding with me. So it was going well enough. But I had a feeling about this night.

Less than an hour away from the restaurant, we were traveling along the side of a large hill, and there was a steep slope upward on our left and a steep slope downward on our right. I came around a bend and saw two strange riders, not from our ranch, standing beside their horses.

"Lakes!" they yelled, gesturing toward the trail.

"What?" I yelled back.

"Slakes!"

"What?" What the heck were slakes?

Oh.

In the middle of the path were two rattlesnakes. I had never seen a rattler up close but from watching at least as many nature shows as the average person, I knew the two we had in front of us were quite large. They were all wrapped up together, furiously either fighting or mating. It was hard to tell which tail went with which head.

With a stern voice I immediately stopped the ride. Some of the horses saw the snakes and started to get nervous. Some of the people did as well. Some in back tried to move up closer to see the snakes, causing the horses in the front of the group to surge forward.

"Everybody keep your horses exactly where they are!" I yelled. "Ellen, Jenny, keep everybody where they are!"

Both Ellen and Jenny looked just as lost as the guests. The snakes were moving so furiously they would occasionally, suddenly move three feet closer to our horses' legs.

I scanned the thirty-five riders. The horses had become tightly packed together and some were still pushing ahead.

"Everybody back it up! Back it up!" I yelled. I then turned Gus and steered him directly into the herd of riders and gave him leg. He hesitated, wondering what I was asking, but I asked him again and he said, *Alright*, and we drove the horses and guests back and created some space between them and the snakes.

Things calmed for a moment. I had to make a decision quickly before the horses got more excited or the snakes got closer.

"What do we do?" Ellen asked.

The path was tight. To the left of me was the side of a mountain, straight up. To the right was a ravine, straight down. The ravine was a possibility. It was thick terrain though. If I got the horses down there, it would not be a definite that we could get them back up. I thought about the possibility of turning the ride around and refunding thirty-five riders.

People waited. Snakes slithered.

I looked down at the bone-bead bracelet. *The one thing that has to happen for sure,* I thought, *no matter what, is not a single horse and rider is going to get hurt.* I needed to not *think* something would work or *hope* something would work, I needed to *know* it would work.

I looked over the situation. I could see a way.

"We're going to take the horses down into the ravine and around the snakes. Follow me," I said.

I took Gus down into the ravine. One by one the group began to follow behind. Once past the snakes I looked for a way back up to the trail, but nothing was presenting itself. I looked behind me at the thirty-five people, some of whom were riding horses for the first time. Only about ten riders had made it down into the ravine so far. I went a little farther and saw a possible way back up to the trail. It wasn't great but it was our best shot.

I asked Gus and with all his might he began climbing out of the ravine. Dirt and rock fell as Gus dug in, breathing hard and grunting as I leaned forward and gave him leg. He fell to his knees as earth gave way around him. I gave him more leg and with a grunt he willed himself back to his feet and pushed on and made it to the top.

I looked behind me at the riders following. "Lean forward, give them leg, and keep it on!" I instructed. One rider made it and then another. Durango fell to his knees with his rider. I looked into Durango's eyes and saw him struggle and fight to get back up, and he did, and he made it. I now had five riders up with me.

I looked again at the remaining line. *There's too many,* I thought. *There's a good chance someone is going to fall.*

"Alright, everybody stop where you are! Those of you down in the ravine keep heading up here. Those of you on the other side, stay there."

I had half my riders on one side of the snakes and the other half on the other side. I could feel the eyes on me. I had only one choice now. I got down off Gus and asked a guest to hold him, and then I went looking for a tree branch. A really *long* tree branch. I found one, and as I approached the rattlers, I tried to remember everything I had ever heard on those National Geographic shows. *Rattlers can only strike out half their length…or was it three-quarters their length?*

I caught a break. As I approached, one of the rattlers slithered away. He became a non-factor. So it was just the one now.

Thirty-five people went quiet. I reached out with the branch…

Bam! The instant the branch touched the snake he shot into his protective coil and the rattle went off with a deep and menacing tone.

"Ooohhhh," the guests said in unison.

I moved back but stayed with the rattler. I tried to softly stick the end of the branch under one of his coils. I worked it in there, and as I lifted the branch, it bent with the thick weight of the snake. I moved it about three feet and the creature slithered off the stick and started toward me. I backed away until I could get the end of the branch under him again. I maneuvered him toward the ravine until he slipped off once more, and just as before, made his way toward me. It seemed like it was a fun game to the snake: I would push him toward the ravine, he would slide off the end of the branch and slither toward me, until I would get him and push him toward the ravine again. After four rounds of this, I got him close to the edge and…

I flung him.

I didn't want to make the mistake of not flinging him enough, so I ended up launching the poor guy. The snake flew as if he had wings. He landed in a bush, thirty feet down into the ravine, none the worse for wear, I guessed.

The riders applauded as I walked back to Gus.

The next morning I got up early. The sky was overcast. The Hollywood streets quiet. Pretty soon I was on the highway, and the Grand Prix and I were putting the miles behind us. And I thought about the new land I was heading into.

I thought about my last days on the ranch and saying goodbye to the horses. It was tougher this time. Gus, Scout, Chief, Smokey. We had worked hard together, and they had been there any time I needed them. They had become close friends, and they had taught me so much.

When I went to see Smokey for the last time, I sat with him a bit. There was nothing to forgive him for, but I asked for his forgiveness for putting him in a situation he wasn't ready to handle. It hadn't affected him much; everybody went back to treating him fairly. He was working in the rides just fine, and when we arrived at the restaurant with the guests he parked himself with the other horses, untied, and stood right with them and didn't move until we were all ready to go. He met the wranglers halfway and offered what he was comfortable doing.

I also knew he had it in him to tie confidently. And something told me that I could be someone who might help a horse like him overcome his fears. I wasn't there yet though.

10 | Harmony

WE THINK SO MUCH about getting the body of the horse to do as we wish. We use every means possible to harness his strength, persuade him to engage his core muscles and push from his mighty hindquarters, to rise high through his back and lift and lighten his shoulders so we may more easily control his power. So that we can say we have him "collected."

Collection is a prized term in modern horse training, what many riders strive for in circle after circle, what they diligently try to achieve. Many different means are used to get the horse to collect, some based on technique—like pushing the horse forward with seat, leg, spur, and crop into the firm contact of the bridle—and some based on mechanical means, such as with the use of tie-downs, side-reins, draw-reins, and martingales. Using seat and leg to engage the horse's impulsion forward while simultaneously restraining his speed with the reins is the most common way. All of these methods have one thing in common: We are trying to get the horse into the position we want him to be in by using physical pressure. We push from the outside-in with no thought as to whether the horse would choose to do it or not.

Most horses' normal head carriage has their necks slightly raised and their heads in a relaxed position, neither vertical or horizontal. When they are curious, worried, scared, or hurting, horses naturally raise their heads higher. They cannot do this when their heads are restricted by mechanical means or with hard hands on the reins. The head then only finds relief when it yields to the pressure forcing it to stay down, where we want it for our purposes.

There is no dance or sport or event in the world where we force someone's head down and celebrate it like we do with horses.

It's true that bits and reins and riding crops are all tools, and tools take on the life of their users. It is in the spirit of the one guiding the horse—his handler, his rider—that the horse truly feels led. We truly can never judge; we don't know the whole story behind a human and a horse and what brought them to a moment together.

But in the eyes of the horse, we can see the difference when he feels good and is inspired in what he is doing, and when he is not.

When the movement comes from the inside—the heart and the soul shaping the body—you see the difference like night and day. The united pride between horse and human beams. When a horse is inspired in what he is doing, he naturally uses his body to the best of his ability. All the strength and grace and collection is right there—the horse strong and stretching and floating of his own accord.

This is natural balance.

When a horse is balanced from the inside-out, it is beautiful. The horse believes in what he is doing, enjoys it, and wants more. You can see this kind of balance in how a horse moves while free in a field with other horses, how gracefully and proudly he carries himself without anybody showing him how to do it. He is balanced over his hindquarters with great strides, his back strong, his neck arched. The art in riding is to try and inspire the horse in such a way that he feels as engaged and proud with you as he does at liberty with herdmates, because then the balance and collection of his body is a natural result of that, without any force necessary.

When there is balance in the souls, minds, and bodies of the human and the horse together, it is unmistakable. Everything they do together looks easy, as if the ability to do what they are doing was in their stars to begin with. And it brings a smile to your face just watching it.

As with everything when it comes to horses, we must find this balance within ourselves first. We must know our horses and respect them as individuals and listen to them and let go of achieving our goals at their expense. We can work together with our horses in a way that they can invest in and enjoy just as much as we do. True balance is when beautiful inner connection produces beautiful outer connection. When our connection to ourselves produces a connection to everything in our lives.

I passed a sign:

Mexico

10 Miles

On either side of me was nothing but the Sonoran Desert and its mesquite trees, sandy ravines, and yellow rock mountains. Giant Saguaro cactus in all shapes and sizes guarded over the landscape with their long arms.

Another sign:

Mexico

1 Mile

I came around a turn and just before the border there was a sign for the ranch beside a small dirt road. The road was set deep into the land like it had been there since the old times and the land had grown up around it. In my rearview mirror I could see the wake of dust rising up from the Grand Prix like a mushroom cloud. The land was dry. It was beautiful sure enough... but a little mean.

Something caught my eye amongst the thick mesquite trees.

There were horses, four or five, free-grazing about a hundred yards from

the road. Heads casually picked up to look at me. Further on were three burros. I drove on and saw three more horses standing beside the road.

I stopped the car to watch them. I had never seen horses free, and it
had a profound effect on me. They were not wild though—they had freeze
brands on their left shoulders. The brand of the Rancho de la Osa.

As I drove into the ranch a man walked out of a building. I stopped the
Grand Prix and got out. He was in his early fifties. He was thin and wore a
baseball hat, eyeglasses, jeans, and tennis shoes. "You must be our new cowboy," he said with a smile and his hand extended. "Welcome to the Rancho."

"Thanks, and you must be Tom," I said with a big smile myself.

"I am. How was your trip?"

"A little longer than I expected, especially on this last road here. I
thought I was going to end up in Mexico."

"Almost. You see that ridge over there?" he pointed to a small ridge a
quarter mile away. "That's Mexico right there."

The ranch was centered around a large adobe hacienda. In front of the
hacienda patio was a beautiful courtyard with colorful plants, many vari-
eties of cactus, and two towering Eucalyptus trees. To either side were a
line of adobe guest rooms and at the far end were the workers quarters
and the horse corrals. Behind the hacienda were Tom and Monica's house
and another house for ranch workers. The architecture was tan and brown,
turquoise and green. The history of the ranch had been preserved and the
culture from which it was created was intact. I was in Mexico and Spain and
America all at the same time.

Tom took me up to his house where Monica was making dinner. She
was a petite woman with red hair and a warm smile. As we ate, they told me
about the land and its buildings, what brought them to owning it, and how
it now worked as a guest ranch.

"We wanted to retire and have an adventure at the same time," said
Monica. "So here we are at the Rancho de la Osa."

"When do the guests start coming and how many are usually here at a time?"

"We open near the end of August, and it varies," she said. "Sometimes we just have five or six guests here, sometimes we're full at forty. We cater to those who want to live the ranch experience as well as eat great food and sleep in a great room with a big fireplace. Most guests stay around a week, and we really get to know them. We want to make it such a good stay for them that the goodbye is hard, you know?"

"The place is magical," added Tom. "You can feel the story behind the architecture and the land."

"How big is the staff?"

"Let's see," pondered Tom. "Two chefs, Jaime and Bill; one office manager, Lydia; two housekeepers who also help with serving at meals, Louis and Maria; a maintenance man, Al; the groundskeepers, Jose and Hector; and the head cowboy, Cody. We usually have three cowboys but right now it's just you and him."

"Have you talked to him about Cody yet?" queried Monica.

"Right, right." There was a pause. "What you have to realize about Cody is," Tom started, "is that, well, he's a great guy, and he's absolutely great with the guests, people love him, but he's…a cowboy. A little rough around the edges."

"He's been here for about a year now and he's a good fit," said Monica.

"He's a great horseman and we love him," added Tom.

"But he likes to drink," Monica added, her eyes dropping down as she said it.

"And he sometimes gets a little…" Tom looked up at the ceiling trying to find the words. "Hard to work with. On a ranch in the middle of nowhere it's like you're living in a one-room house with everyone. It can get a little tight sometimes."

"I think he's out to the bar tonight," said Monica looking down at her plate. "You'll meet him tomorrow."

At the end of the night I was told where my room was, right down by the corrals, and given a small electric lantern and the warning: *If you see a stick moving in front of you, it's not a stick.* There were no lights on in any of the buildings. The place felt like a ghost town. It was hot. The honest, straightforward heat of the Southwest. As I walked by the Grand Prix, I gave the dusty car a much-deserved pat on the hood for another weighed-down, hard-won drive. I made it to my room and opened the door. It was small with a bathroom and a back door. I opened the back door to see where it led.

Horses. The door led right into a corral. I stepped out and there I was, so close to them I just reached out my hand to a bay horse, standing nearby. There were two others with him. A dark-colored horse with one blue eye, and in the far corner, a tall, gangly sorrel with a long white blaze.

I heard a loud rumbling noise approaching the front gate of the ranch. The rumbling slowly grew louder until it was within the compound. Right about the time it would be passing my front door, it slowed and then ended. I went back inside my room and waited.

I heard a vehicle door open and shut and footsteps over gravel to the cement walkway in front of my room. There was a jingling with each purposeful step. Spurs.

A very deliberate knock on the door. I opened it.

"Howdy. I'm Cody Lake. Welcome to the La Osa Ranch."

His first words were said with warmth and a big smile as he looked me directly in the eye and extended his hand. He was in his late thirties. A medium-build man with a curly goatee and brown, slightly curly hair that stuck out from under a dirty white Stetson. He had on a long sleeve, button-up shirt (also dirty), Wrangler jeans, and leather boots that looked like they had seen many a ride. And the spurs.

"How's yer trip?" he asked. "You were comin' from out California way, right?"

"Yeah, California. Long ride but I made it."

"Well, alright then. It's good to have ya here. We're outta season right now as I'm sure ya know but we've plenty of work that'll keep us busy."

He was full of expression in his words and gestures and eyes. He was charismatic in an immediate sense. He had also been drinking and had a glow on.

"Ya own a saddle do ya?" he asked.

"No."

"That's alright. There's some good saddles out the back. We got almost fifty horses here, and we'll find a good one for ya in the mornin' as well. We'll set ya up straight."

"Thanks, that sounds great. When and where should I start?"

He thought for a second. "Well, how about this. I'm ridin' out in the mornin' to gather some horses been out a while. You wanna ride with me?"

"Yeah, sure."

"Alright. Let's say meet me out back at the corrals around six. That'll give me time to get some stuff done before then."

"Sounds great."

He then looked me right in the eye. "You'll find I'm a hard worker and a straight-shooter. If you ever have something you want to say or talk about I don't wantcha hesitatin'."

"Well, I'm real happy to be here and I'm ready to go to work with you, learn from you, and do whatever you need me to do."

Cody looked away modestly. "Aw heck, we'll just work and have a good time. This job is too much fun not to have a good time. You'll learn from me, and I'll learn from you."

That night I lay down on top of the bed with no covers or pillows. It was too hot for anything. It wasn't the most comfortable of beds, but it was the first bed I had slept on in half a year. With the windows open the sounds of the desert night poured in about the room. I couldn't sleep. I was nervous. I wanted to not just be able to do the job I had been hired for, I wanted to do it well.

I didn't want to let anyone down, including myself.

I heard the sound of Cody's truck driving out to the corrals a little after five. The horses called to him. Everything was quiet until the birds announced the sun was rising. I put the bone-bead bracelet on and looked at my eyes in the mirror. I was clean-shaven, wide-eyed, and ready. At six I came out of my room wearing a long-sleeve, button-up shirt, the very stiff brand-new Wrangler jeans, my boots, and my brown Stetson.

I made my way around the corner to the corrals and there they were. Horses of all sizes and colors, eating hay inside the mesquite fencing. Cody was already getting up on his horse, the bay I met the night before outside my back door. He had on his white Stetson and big-heeled cowboy boots with the spurs. He wore a pair of dark leather chinks. Around his neck was a blue cowboy scarf. The saddle was fine-crafted, worn-in, with a lariat coiled and tied near the horn. When Cody swung a leg over and sat down it was as if the cowboy clicked into place. He immediately looked like he perfectly fit the saddle, the horse.

But when Cody looked at me this time there was no warmth.

"When I say be out here at six that means be out with yer horse saddled and ready to go at six. This may be a guest ranch, but I run a cowboy operation here. I realize you ain't got much experience in that, but I got things that gotta git done. I can't be waitin' on ya."

He then turned his horse and trotted toward the gate, opened it without looking back, and took off at a quick lope and disappeared into the trees of the Sonoran Desert.

I stood there.

Not the best way to start.

What was I doing here? A cowboy? Maybe I had reached too far on this one. I walked into the tack room. Saddles and bridles lined the walls. With no clear idea of anything else to do I started cleaning. I thought about what I had done wrong exactly. I was out there right at six. Was that some sort of cowboy test?

An hour later I heard the sound of hooves moving over the ground and the sound of a human voice behind them. "Come on! Come on, horses! Hup! Hup!"

Five horses were trotting back to the ranch with Cody behind them, guiding them in. He brought them up beside the big corral and then loped past them and skillfully opened the gate from horseback, rode back and guided the horses in and closed the gate behind them. The whole thing looked rehearsed.

Cody rode up to where I was standing by the door of the tack room.

"Cody, I'm sorry," I said sincerely. "I should have been out here earlier."

"Well, I was thinkin' I hadn't been quite fair with ya. Nothing was yer fault," he said as he got down from the bay. "Come on. Let's get ya a horse."

He walked toward the small pen my back door led to. In it were the blue-eyed horse and the tall sorrel with the white blaze. Cody went to the sorrel and placed the loop of his lariat loosely around the horse's neck. He then led him out of the pen and dropped the lariat to the ground and the horse stood there quietly.

When I first saw the sorrel, my thought was that he was a little gangly and awkward looking, with his tall, thin body and narrow neck and head. He didn't look very strong. Didn't look like anything much at all really.

All in all, I was a little let down that the sorrel was going to be my horse that day.

"This is Alto. He's been here fer a while, he's around ten or so. A good horse. A good ranch horse."

I walked over to Alto. Our eyes met. We studied each other. After taking a moment to size me up he looked away, unimpressed. Apparently, I didn't look like much at all to him either.

I went into the tack room and picked the saddle I liked. It was old, not much to it in looks, but I liked something about it. I got myself a bridle, and in no time, I had Alto ready.

"Alright, let's go, cowboy," Cody said as he placed a foot in a stirrup and got back up on the bay. I followed, swinging onto Alto.

"Is that your horse?" I asked.

"Jake here is owned by the ranch. When I got here nobody was ridin' him. He was too dangerous they all said. They kept him all by himself in a small pen."

We rode through the gate and out into the desert. Cody immediately started talking to me about the ranch, which gates to go through, the difference in the corrals, how Tom and Monica liked things done, about the land. He didn't stop talking or smiling. The way he talked, the swagger to his words, made you feel at ease and had you enjoying being around him. He would walk Jake for a ways and then trot a little or take him up into a lope, and I would follow on Alto, just off to his side. I had never seen anyone ride like Cody. He rode the horse softly and fluidly with no discernible cues or movement in his seat. It was riding without any noticeable riding.

There were no trails. We were just openly riding the land, over rocky hills, through fields of yellow grass, and down along dry, sandy riverbeds called arroyos. I was amazed at the surefootedness of the horses.

"This land is rough," said Cody. "It's desert but it's the most floral desert in the world, and everything has thorns. Ya got yer grasslands here, but mostly it's all ups and downs, sand and rocks and trees, mesquite mostly, with a lot of arroyos made from the monsoons. There ain't no water except for a few little waterin' holes I'll show ya. Ya gotta be dang careful out here. With the rattlers, scorpions, spiders, thorns, and sun, everything out here will bite ya, sting ya, stick ya, or burn ya."

He was right. Everything seemed on the defensive in an offensive sort of way. Prickly pear cactus with thin, piercing thorns; barrel cactus with hooking, talon-like thorns; the yucca plant with razor sharp edges; and the mesquite trees with their rugged inch-long thorns. You couldn't brush up against anything.

"So, you let the horses graze out here on their own?" I asked.

"Yes sir. We have almost fifty head, mostly Quarter Horses, some Mustangs, some Belgians, a few Mexican horses. About half are in right now, the others we currently have out on the range. Some stay close like the ones I brought in this morning, others go out pritty far. The Rancho de la Osa used to own the whole valley, but now it has just around five hundred acres. We're surrounded by the Buenos Aires National Wildlife Refuge, though, and they have near one hundred and twenty thousand acres of open land they let us use and our horses wander all over it. Sometimes you'll find horses ten or twelve miles away from the ranch. Whatever horses are out we make sure we lay eyes on 'em every week or two to know they're okay and so they remember they're domesticated."

"How many are you looking for today?"

"There's a group of eight or ten I ain't seen fer a while."

We rode on for about an hour and I had no idea where we were or in which direction the ranch was. Cody stopped now and then to examine tracks or to scan the horizon with his binoculars. I dove right into it, scouting for tracks myself.

After about two hours of riding Cody led us into a grove of trees and to a hidden watering hole. We sat atop the horses while they drank, the sun pouring down on us. I wiped the sweat from my forehead with my shirtsleeve.

"A lot of tracks here," I said.

"Pritty much everything in a four-mile radius will make the time to come here. This is the biggest watering hole for a while. If you're lucky you can catch horses here gettin' a drink."

We followed a line of tracks leading away from the watering hole that Cody thought looked fresh. I couldn't tell the difference. We came to a thick forest of mesquite we had to pick our way through. Then it opened up into rolling fields of grass with scattered patches of trees.

"So, yer from Maine. What's that like?"

"Maine is nice. It's actually got some similar qualities to the Western states, as far as the way of life. Where are you from?"

"Me? I'm from Iowa. I lit out after high school to be a cowboy, and that's what I've been doing since, workin' from ranch to ranch."

We rode on. Cody led the way, cutting through the land as if he knew every inch. If it was open, we were loping, side by side. If it was thick with brush, we walked, picking our way through.

"You see, I'm also a cowboy poet," Cody said squinting at me from under the dirty brim off his hat.

"Really? I'd like to read some of your stuff some time."

"Read it? Well…it's not exactly meant to be read. Cowboy poetry is a spoken thing, ya see."

We came across a line of empty water bottles littered about with dirty shirts and sneakers beside them.

"Mojados," Cody said. "You always gotta be on the look fer mojados and banditos."

"Mojados?" I asked.

"The illegals that come across the border. They say there's like a hundred a day coming across these parts. The banditos are the ones that camp out here and ambush 'em, knowing they have all their money and life's possessions with 'em. The ranch's take on it all is we don't bother them and they don't bother us. With the guests riding with us and all, it's kinda how it needs to be. You'll see the border patrol out as well, but they mostly stick to the roads. We notify them if we see anything and —" Cody stopped Jake and looked up ahead. "Hey, what's that out there? You seein' that?"

I looked hard and saw nothing but hills and trees.

Without any noticeable cue Cody took Jake up into a lope. I followed with Alto. We moved fast for a ways until Cody came to a quick halt and pulled out his binoculars.

"Down in that little dip, you see 'em?" He pointed but I saw nothing. He passed me the binoculars. "Just past that second ridge off to the left of that grove-a trees."

I scanned the ridge with the binoculars, and I saw what looked like a tail swishing under a tree but I couldn't be sure. It appeared to be a good half mile away.

"That's them," Cody said excitedly. "Come on."

We rode out wide to the east of the horses. I soon forgot in what direction they were but Cody seemed like he knew where he was going. We arrived on a small hilltop. Below us were twelve horses spread out grazing and enjoying the morning sun.

"You ever brought in horses before?" Cody asked without taking his eyes off them. He was serious now.

"No."

"Okay. They're gonna run. We don't want 'em to but they will. Especially with that gray leading the pack. They've been living the good life and they're probably not gonna want to come in. We're just gonna stay with 'em so we don't lose 'em. If we lose 'em we might not find 'em again today and then this day's work is all fer not."

Jake started to get excited. Alto started to dance underneath me.

"Don't feel like you have to help or keep up," Cody said, holding Jake back. "It's gonna git Western and I don't wantcha hurtin' yerself. Just get yer deep seat, keep yer mind in the middle of the saddle, and ride the ride."

We slowly walked in behind the horses, and one by one their heads raised. We got within fifty yards when one of the horses, a tall gray mare, turned to look at us. I could see the wildness in her eye, unblinking as it followed our intentions.

She turned and started moving. The others followed.

Cody slowly followed on Jake. I followed off to their side.

The gray walked calmly with her herd behind. Cody softly rode up one side and guided them in the direction he wanted. He whistled sharply to get their attention. All of the horses had one eye on us. As Cody worked one side, I went to the other, and together we kept them moving the way we wanted. It was going easy, so far.

Up ahead I saw a small dip to the land, and without ever bringing horses in before, I could sense what was going to happen.

The gray led them down into the dip, and they all broke into a trot as they ran up the other side. They then stayed in the trot. Heads started tossing. Tails swished. My nerves, like they were tied to the horses, started to build. I reached up and pulled my hat tight. Choked up on the reins and set my feet deeper into the stirrups. I looked down at the bone-bead bracelet on my wrist.

The energy was no longer containable. The gray took off.

"Here we go," called Cody.

Twelve horses sprinted across the yellow grasslands as fast as they could go with the gray mare in the lead. Hooves thundered across the ground. Dirt and dust flew back at us like rain and fog as we galloped after them. Cody stayed right with them on the running Jake. The man rode beautifully. Alto and I were right there as well. I was already going twice as fast as I had ever gone on a horse.

I was all over the saddle. The land was twisty and bumpy, and we were really moving. I stayed calm, kept a soft feel on the reins, and tried to sit Alto as deeply as I could.

We approached a mesquite forest, and in seconds the escaping horses fell into a line and disappeared underneath the branches at a full run. Without slowing or hesitating, Cody ducked the branches and he and Jake disappeared after the herd.

All that was left in front of me was a cloud of dust. As Alto and I galloped up to the mesquite, I hesitated. I thought about easing back—and staying alive.

Alive…and the same. Nothing about me would change.

"Let's go, Alto!" I leaned forward, loosened the reins, touched both legs to his sides, and we charged into the trees and dust.

There was no riding straight anymore, it was all cutting and turning around the trees, ducking branches and leaning from one side to the other. We weren't cantering or loping or galloping—we were *running*, down one side of an arroyo and up the other, taking a straightaway as fast as we could before hitting the brakes for a turn. Some branches weren't duckable and there was nothing to do but close my eyes and shield myself with an arm. Mesquite thorns sliced into my hands, neck, and face. I tasted blood.

I couldn't see the horses or Cody, all I had was the trail of dust. Everything was silent except for the sound of Alto's hooves moving assuredly over the uneven terrain and his breath steadily puffing as we went as fast as we could in and around the trees. The more I thought I was behind, the more I asked Alto for more, and the more he gave. We were digging with all we had.

Suddenly I saw hooves in the hot dust up ahead, kicking out, running hard. The band of horses started appearing one by one in front of me until we emerged from the mesquite and out onto the flats. Everything was open and clear…and I was right behind them.

"Yeehaaaaa!"

It was Cody. He was just off to the side of the herd. He rode right up next to me. His eyes full of the excitement of the moment. "Can you believe we get paid for this!" he shouted. Joy shining in his face.

The horses started to spread out and he yelled for me to cover one side while he worked the other. With a job to do I stopped thinking and just worked as hard as I could. There was a lot of running and slowing down, cutting back and running again. The runaways finally slowed a little. It was as if they had given it their best shot, and when they saw we were still with them, they gave up. The gray mare slowed to a walk and the herd followed, nice and easy.

My heart slowed down and then my breath. I finally had a moment to think. I patted Alto heartily on his sweaty neck. My cheeks felt the strain of a big smile that was uncontainable.

"Whew!" yelled Cody. "Good ridin', partner. Good ridin'!"

By early afternoon we had the horses in. Cody rode up and opened the gate, and I guided the herd into the large pen. I then followed Cody as we rode right through the ranch and to the office. Monica came out to greet us.

"Well, they gave us a run but we got 'em," said Cody proudly. "We were runnin' so fast we pritty dang near left our shadows behind."

"Great," said Monica with a smile while shading her eyes. "How did you do out there?" she asked me.

Cody, smiling, turned to hear my answer.

"Well…I had a lot of fun," I said.

Cody laughed. "I tell ya what," he said. "This guy is a keeper. He rode the best I've seen anybody ride that land." He looked right at me, squinting his eyes with a slight nod of his head the way he did when saying something he meant. "You couldn't-a done better."

As I unsaddled the sweaty Alto, I couldn't stop thanking him. I couldn't believe how much of himself he had given. I let my thanks show to him, in the way I patted his neck, in the way I talked to him, in my eyes. As I looked at his legs, I noticed the scratches and cuts from the many thorns of the desert, with a few still stuck where they had dug in.

"We gotta look after these guys after every ride and doctor up their legs," Cody said as he came out from the tack room with a pail of warm water, a cloth, and some antibiotic. "The care of our horses comes before all else."

The sun was out, there wasn't a cloud in the sky, and it must have been around a hundred degrees. Cody's spurs happily jingled with each step as we walked through the ranch on our way to get some lunch. Jose and Hector were working on a fence, Monica was sitting outside the office doing paperwork, Al was going into one of the guest rooms to fix something. The ranch was like its own little world. Cody stopped to say hi to everyone.

In the afternoon we walked out to the corrals to mingle with the horses. One by one Cody talked to me about each of them. "That's Kahlua, a good big horse, but a little skittish. That there is Amarillo. He's good for pritty much anything. Buttermilk over there, he's for beginners. Tamayo is fast and a little wild."

Later we got into his old and rusted white truck to go to town. Sasabe amounted to a general store, a post office, a church, a mechanic's garage, and a bar. Cody took me to the general store first. His spurs were still jangling along with him, and his white Stetson was set back upon his head. He walked in like he owned the place.

"Cody!" said the woman behind the counter. "We haven't seen you for two days. Just where have you been?"

"Out looking fer horses. How have you been, Miss Debbie?"

"Good. Who's that with you?"

"This is my new partner."

"Is this the new cowboy that was coming to the Rancho?"

"Yup. And he just brought in twelve horses with me at a dead run from ten miles out."

Cody bought his tobacco and a twelve-pack of beer. Next, we went to see Mike the mechanic across the street. Then Gloria, who ran the post office. Everybody in town knew Cody and seemed to like him. We picked up the mail for the ranch and then got back into his truck.

"Pop me one of those beers, cowboy, and get one fer yerself," he said, "and let's go look fer some horses."

We drove north, and then Cody took a left onto a bumpy dirt road and we cut into the Sonora. It was late afternoon now and shadows started to stretch over the land and the air cooled. It was a great time for this part of the world. Cody had the steering wheel in one hand and a beer in the other. He drove up a small hill and parked the truck. He left his cassette player going. George Strait sang out to the desert.

"Sometimes you can see where some horses are at from here," he said.

"Are there still a lot out?"

"About twenty-five or so." He opened another beer and passed me another even though I had a bit left. "What d'ya think of ol' Alto today?"

"Man, that horse—"

"He worked his dang heart out fer ya, didn't he?"

"He sure did. And Jake, man, he was flying. I didn't think he could move as fast as he did."

"Ol' Jake, he's just relaxed now. And when a horse is relaxed, you'd be amazed at what he can do."

"Do you ever take the guests out to bring in horses?"

"Well, my philosophy is that if the guests are up for it, we should get them right involved with the workings of the ranch and that means gathering the cattle and horses. Other times we just gotta keep it to little bumpety-bump rides. Sometimes that's all people want, sometimes that's all they can do."

We talked about the ranch for an hour before heading back. He dropped me off in front of my room. Through the talking while riding and the talking while driving I felt like I had known the man for years. We shook hands and I walked into my room, took my hat and boots off, put the bone-bead bracelet on the desk and collapsed on the bed, spent. I could feel the sweat and dirt burning into the abrasions that had been scraped raw on the insides of my knees.

I felt I had just lived a life in one day. And there was no past here. This life was new. No Allison, no Karen, no lost finger.

Each day started with feeding horses around five-thirty. It was dark and we moved around using electric lanterns until the sun came up, greeting us every day like clockwork with a beautiful Arizona sunrise.

We then either rode out with Jake and Alto and looked for horses or worked the horses that were in at the ranch. Cody showed me how he liked to work with them, free at first, talking about how it was important to leave a horse a choice, because then when he chose to work with you, *all* of the horse came with that—his full try, his confidence, and all his strength. He spoke of the thoughts of the horse, how if you have the horse's body with you but not his mind, then sooner or later the horse will go where his thoughts are, leaving you. But if you have the horse's thoughts with you, then his body will be with you, one hundred percent of the time.

"It's all in yer sense of it, how you think of it. Then it's in yer feel of it, how you apply it," Cody said. "You wanna get so you have a sense for it, you know in yer mind what you wanna do, and then a soft feel in how you apply it, in yer technique."

He talked of each horse as an individual and about finding the trust with that specific horse. "You find that connecting point on the ground, and then it's all downhill from there."

We would sometimes ride five to ten horses a day, getting them ready before the guests were due to come. Everything was dusty and sweaty under the hundred-degree sun. Cody taught me a lot in each ride. He thought I was a natural, saying he could see my ability and passion for it all, for the horses and for the connection I wanted to make with each of them. He liked the way I rode but said I was "trying" too much in my riding. He worked with me on how to ride more easily in my balance and in the motion of my hips and pelvic bone, following the horse's movement rather than relying on the stirrups and the seat of the saddle.

In those first weeks, if I had time off, I spent it working horses or riding out on Alto to get a better understanding of the land. There was a spot close to the ranch that had a perfect balance of all the terrain in the Sonora, and I used it to practice how to ride the land at fast speeds. I came to call it "The Training Ground."

One day we had to give the horses their annual immunization shots. Cody got Jose to help us, and the plan was that Jose and I would rope the horses in the pen, and Cody would give them the shots while we held them.

Cody knew I couldn't rope, but I couldn't be the guy giving the shots, so I had to try my best at it. I did okay, but Jose ended up doing most of the work.

"I guess that's what we gotta work on next with ya," Cody said, smiling.

So every day after that, when we got the day's work done, Cody helped me with my roping. We stood side by side and roped two fence posts. When I started to get good, we had roping contests, best out of ten. I sometimes got eight or nine. Cody never missed.

One day I went to give back the lariat I had been using.

"Why don'tcha keep it," he said.

"Cody, no I don't wanna—"

"You'll need it and I got other lariats just as good."

"Thanks."

"And you and Alto seem to get along pritty well. You like him, do ya?"

"Alto is the most amazing horse I've been on." I looked Cody right in the eye. "He has strong heart," I said.

Cody squinted at me. "Well, we'll keep him in the pen with Jake. Keep our two horses there so we have 'em whenever we need."

And for the first time in my life, I had the feeling of having my own horse.

"Well, if I didn't feel so good, I'd feel bad!" Cody yelled at the beginning of each ride with the guests.

He had a way with people. Cody made them feel comfortable right away in his humor, charm, and swagger. He was a real cowboy loving every second of his life, and it was infectious—ask anyone standing within fifty yards of him.

The guests started coming, with most staying anywhere from three days to a week. We did two rides a day, each one lasting around two hours. Cody led and I did whatever he asked. Most of the time we let the guests ride as they liked, as long as they listened to us. Cody hated everybody riding in a line. He kept each outing alive and varied, going in different directions each day. I started to know the land, which allowed us to sometimes split the ride up with Cody taking the more advanced riders to go look for horses while I rode with the beginners.

The evenings were spent in the ranch cantina. It was good size, with a piano, a fireplace, a refrigerator full of beer, and a row of tequilas behind the bar. Cody and I would meet the guests there after the afternoon ride. In Cody's words, "we rode hard and then we played hard." He held court, the center of attention, and the guests hung on his every word.

"And you've lived your whole life as a cowboy?" Martin, a guest from England, asked Cody.

"Yes, sir. You see being a cowboy ain't a job, it's a way of life."

He would have everybody feeling like there was no place else on earth they would rather be. The evening would turn into a late night and that would turn into fuzzy heads come morning.

I talked a lot with the guests. There was nothing I wouldn't do to make their experience on the ranch a great one. My favorite thing seemed to be helping the people who were nervous. There was something about the fact that they were fearful yet still drawn to horses, wanting to ride, that attracted me. I wanted to help them through that fear so they could experience for themselves what was changing my life.

"Where you wanna take 'em today, Roy?" Cody would yell to me as we rode out from the ranch with the guests. He had taken to calling me Roy, after Roy Rogers, and he did it in a very warm way. The guests loved it. They enjoyed the dynamic between us, the cowboy and the apprentice, and how we worked with each other and played off each other.

The best way to describe these rides with the guests is that everybody was happy. I didn't know who these people were back in the real world, but at the ranch they were good, happy people.

One day we stopped at one of the watering holes. We dismounted and let the horses drink, then tied them to nearby trees. Everybody found a place to lie down and relax. It was *real* relaxation.

I hadn't talked to any of my friends from home in a long time. I hadn't called Mom for a while. The Grand Prix had a thick layer of dust on it from where it had sat, unused, for the past two months. My days with Allison felt distant, a long-ago time in a faraway place. My life, *this* life, was completely new.

On the way home, we came across six horses grazing in a small patch of grass on the side of a rocky hill. Cody wanted to push them a little closer to the ranch. The guests waited in silence as Cody and I looked the situation over.

"Lucy, Jane, Jason…ride with me," said Cody. The three of them rode up beside him with excitement in their eyes. "Roy, you ride drag with the others."

Cody walked Jake up behind the small band of horses and gave instructions to the guests on how they were going to move them. My riders and I trailed behind and watched. Cody had everybody spread out, and on his signal, they started toward the horses. The herd started running a little, and Cody and his riders kept with them. It was great to see.

"Wow. I would give anything to be able to do that," said Martin.

I saw how Cody had worked this. He knew we would come across those horses after we left the watering hole. And they didn't need to be pushed closer to the ranch. But just "coming across" them and then spontaneously putting the guests to work was making the day special. They were getting to be cowboys.

That night we had a cookout with all the ranch workers and guests. Cody, dressed up in his cowboy best, tended the grill while I served drinks. After the cookout we met in the cantina. I popped open beers and made margaritas. Everybody mingled, choosing whether to sit in on the conversation at the bar or sit out on the benches in the courtyard, feeling the cool breeze under the stars.

"Hey, Cody, how about you recite one of your fine poems for these folks," said Tom.

"Aw, I'm not so sure they'd wanna hear that."

"Oh, come on, John Wayne," taunted Martin. "Are you a cowboy or not?"

Cody laughed as he stood up from his seat. Everything went quiet. He stood there for a moment and then closed his eyes as if trying to remember…not the words, but a feeling. His head dipped down. When he brought it back up, he began speaking.

I was out on ol' Ranger,
checking the north fence, mending a post,
thinking about what being a cowboy meant to me,
what mattered the most…

His eyes squinted from underneath his hat brim. His hands made small and then grand motions. He didn't just speak the words…he lived them. He talked of the freedom in the life of a cowboy. And the loneliness that can be beneath it all.

Lived my life mostly all alone,
never laid down roots long enough, to have a home…

People from all over the world silently watched this man and nobody blinked. His words rose and fell, leaving their emotion hanging heavy about the room. For about two minutes he spoke until he came to the end…

a ranch, some horses,
a lovin' family around me...
it just sounds so dang pritty,
and would have this cowboy feelin' so happy.

His eyes closed as he finished the poem and his words faded away like the dust from runaway horses.

The next morning we took the guests out for a sunrise ride. I met Cody around four-thirty to feed and saddle horses. The guests, red-eyed and bed-headed, came out around five and we rode out from the ranch in the dark. After an hour we came to the top of a hill and waited for it to start.

An Arizona sunrise is special. It's sharp and mythical with colors paintings try to find but can't. Great to see however you see it…but we were on horses.

After, as we rode home, Cody stopped and pointed to something up ahead. Mojados, ten of them, made their way through the desert as if out for a casual hike. They looked like homeless people, which is exactly what they were. You could sense the plight about them. Giving up one life for the chance of a better one, everything left behind except what could fit into a small backpack.

This was familiar to me.

In the afternoon we rode in the arena. Cody talked to the guests about the relationship between horse and rider, how it's based on trust, not force, and how when a horse trusts you there's nothing he won't do for you. He demonstrated this by slipping Jake's bridle off while he was riding him, then draping a lead rope around the horse's neck. They loped and stopped on a dime.

I watched closely as he rode. He guided Jake with his seat and leg and then with just the softest touch to the rope, gently massaging it on the horse's neck. It was clear how Jake wasn't feeling cues, he was feeling Cody. Most of the time the rope was so loose it wasn't even touching the bay. Jake didn't look any different than when he had a bridle on. Actually, he looked better.

Cody jumped down and handed the lead rope to me. "Mount up, Roy." It was my first time on Jake, and the moment I was on him all these thoughts shot into my mind from what I was feeling from him. Willing, at the ready, thoughtful. Smart and crisp. Wanting to do what I was going to ask, all in a business-like manner. There was no fooling around with him.

We moved forward. I had never felt a horse so sensitive. He listened and I rode with ease, but I was hesitant. *The horse had nothing on his head.* We loped and I felt a world I had not seen yet.

A horse moves differently when he is free.

I got down and passed the lead line back to Cody. The look in my eye registered in his. I wanted more. I also realized how far my own personal horsemanship had to go. There was a huge difference in how Cody and I rode. He was all feel, you couldn't see what he was doing. I was mechanical and giving noticeable cues.

This was the sense and the feel he had spoken of. Sensing who the horse was at heart and having the feel to connect with him and guide him as softly as possible, with as much freedom as possible.

The next morning we had the horses saddled early. We were taking the guests out to bring in horses.

"Where's Buttermilk?" asked Martin. It was his last day as a guest and Buttermilk was the horse he had been riding.

"Buttermilk isn't going out today," replied Cody. "We're going to look for horses and he can't keep up."

Martin looked at me. I shrugged my shoulders.

"So, I'm not going?" he asked.

"Oh yer going. Yer just takin' Jake," answered Cody.

Martin was shocked. Jake was Cody's horse. The cowboy's horse.

Cody rode Chino and he took Martin and the advanced riders out to gather horses while I took the riders who were looking for a quiet ride. When Cody's group came back I could tell it had been good. Martin was beaming. As he told the story of his ride to the other guests, there was Cody in the background, unsaddling the horses, smiling.

That afternoon after we were done for the day, I took Alto out to the riding arena and prepared to try to ride him bridleless.

"Slow down," Cody said as he came walking up to me.

"I know, I know," I said. "But I want to work on this bridleless riding."

"You can't rush this stuff, Roy. It takes time. You can't force it. You have to just be around horses as much as you can and let it soak into ya. You can't go wrong by taking it slow. Rushing with horses only gets ya in trouble. Rushing with horses breaks the connection. Rushing with horses is what got yer finger taken off."

I smiled and looked away for a second. Then looked back at him. "Yeah, I get it. I understand," I said. I put the bridle on Alto. I still had a lot of work to do.

Guests came and went. I started to find a rhythm and feel to the job, getting up early and working hard straight through the day with the horses, the guests, and the ranch work. After a while I forgot about *trying* to be a cowboy and just did the job. Soon my leather boots were scuffed up, my jeans were faded, and my Stetson was sweat-stained.

I took a lot of rides out on my own. Often, Cody and I would both go with the group and then split up halfway through the ride and meet up again somewhere. It worked well because of how alive and spontaneous the rides were. There were sunrise rides and sunset rides, lunch rides and whole day rides. Herding horses, herding cattle.

On our free days Cody and I would ride out together and gather horses. With the guests around usually one of us had to stay and take care of them while the other went searching. I usually had to handle the guest rides.

One night Cody came up to me while we were in the cantina.

"I was gonna ride out in the morning to bring some horses in but thought I'd ride with the guests instead. You think you can go out and get 'em?" he asked me.

Alto and I rode out of the ranch as the sun was coming up. Around three miles out I checked a watering hole, but it was deserted. I then rode straight northward through the mesquite forest, stopping at one point to watch a rattlesnake slither in front of us. We came out of the forest and rode through some flatland and over the hills and down into the valleys and arroyos and in through patches of trees scattered about the land.

What a great time this was.

I would talk with Alto and then I would be quiet. It was just the two of us in this world. My heart stirred. I felt alive. The quiet out there with nothing but the sound of a horse's steps. I felt an overwhelming connection to Alto for all I was feeling. At one point he turned his head to look back at me. I extended my boot out to his nose. He nuzzled it.

It was hard to visually spot the horses, they blended in so well with the land. But after stopping at a high point on a hill I caught a glimpse of what looked to be a bush that moved in the distance. It was a little black speck among some trees, but it moved.

"Good job, cowboy," Cody said as he opened the gate for me and I brought six horses into the ranch that had been missing for a while.

I felt good. I had done the job that needed to get done. In a short time, Cody and I had become close, and I was glad I didn't disappoint him.

As time went by, I went out more and more to gather horses alone. One day I guided in ten on my own from five miles out. Sometimes I came up with nothing. There was so much land to cover.

I was drinking pretty much every night. Cody led the way every afternoon. "We love our beer," he would say to the guests. People got the craziest they had in years. Doctors and lawyers, husbands and wives, fathers and mothers all dancing on the bar, all loving the cowboy life. And before he got too drunk Cody always stood up and recited a couple of poems. And everybody loved it. Then he swiped his hat off his head and placed it against his heart and extended his hand to all the ladies, one by one, and they smiled and laughed as they danced with him while their husbands took pictures.

Every day we worked hard then partied hard with the guests. It took a toll. I came back to my room at the end of the day, dirt and sweat pasted over my hands and face, and I was as tired as tired could be.

One afternoon I came into my room after a hard day's work and looked in the mirror. I had a beard. My face was tanned, dry, and weathered. My eyes older.

The ranch had three burros that roamed free. They were very friendly and never wandered far. One day while we were out on a ride a neighboring rancher came riding up to talk to Cody. One of the burros had broken his leg.

Cody rode out that afternoon and brought back Armendito, who was hopping on three legs. His left front leg was bent and swollen at the fetlock area. Cody splinted it as best he could.

"There's no way fer him to stay off it, ya see," he said frustrated as he wrapped the splint. "It's just not gonna stay straight long enough fer anything."

Armendito seemed bewildered, like a young kid who had done something wrong but couldn't understand what, looking all around for clues. He stood there with his head low and his eyes sunken in a mix of wonder and failure.

When Tom heard he came out immediately. He loved all his animals.

"It doesn't look good, Tom," said Cody.

"Well, yeah, but we're not going to put him down until we know for sure."

"Tom...I think it's—"

"We're going to wait. I know my animals and the look in his eye says he is not ready to go yet."

Over the next days we took care of Armendito as best we could, changing bandages and resetting the broken leg pretty much every morning. I went in to feed him and pretty soon I was piling new hay on old. The flies swarmed the burro. He made no attempt to fend them off. The look in his eye had changed to something different now. He looked mad at the world.

Cody became very frustrated. He thought the burro was suffering. I went into Armendito's stall every day and tried to see an improvement, but I never did. One night Cody and I were at the Sasabe bar. It was just the two of us with the bartender sitting behind the bar popping open the cans as we drank.

"You think I wanna kill that animal?" he said sharply.

"No, Cody, I—"

"Have you ever put down an animal?"

"No."

"Well, it sure as hell ain't something you ever wanna do! It's the last damn thing I want! I know Tom loves that animal, but all that burro is doing is suffering!"

The next day everybody agreed on what had to be done. Cody walked up to me as I stood by Armendito's stall. He had a pistol holstered at his side.

"I didn't wanna have to ask ya, but can ya help me?"

"Yes," I said.

Cody led him out. The burro labored, hopping on three legs, trying at first but slowing down more and more until he completely refused to move. Cody kept trying to get him to move to no avail. The burro would not take one more step. Cody let out a strained and frustrated sigh and stopped asking Armendito to follow him. He looked to the ground while breathing heavy, the brim of his hat hiding his face.

After a long silence he pointed to a mesquite tree. "Go to that mesquite yonder and break off a branch."

I did as he asked.

"When I ask him to move," he said, "you're gonna have to make him go from behind."

I stepped behind Armendito and prepared myself. Cody asked for him to move and when he wouldn't I tapped him on his rear.

"More," Cody said.

I tapped him again, then again…

"It's gonna have to be more firm," he said.

I hesitated. I then used the branch just a bit firmer and like lightning Armendito shot a kick out at me. It came within a foot of my stomach.

"Look out, don't get killed," said Cody. "I know it's a dang thing to be doin' but yer gonna have to keep at it."

I used the stick again, trying to just urge Armendito on. Eventually he hobbled forward. We went through the gate and into the desert. Cody pulled. Armendito resisted. I used the stick. On it went. His leg dragging on the ground. His eye back on me, not angry, but disappointed.

The horses came out to the edge of the big corral. All of them. They lined up in an orderly fashion, and they stared at us and what we were doing. They didn't look like horses anymore, they looked like judges, all with an equal say. I didn't want to look at them, but they looked at me, neither condoning nor condemning, because it was something they had judged on a long time ago, and now the verdict was just a shadow behind their eyes. I felt so distant from them. This was a spike to my heart.

The death march pushed on. It was all just a mess, what had to be done and how we were doing it. It was so hot. Sweat streamed off our faces and sizzled into the desert sand. Every now and then Cody's and my eyes would meet, but like it was forbidden, we immediately looked away.

After half an hour of trying to move him to the ranch graveyard where other animals had been taken through the years, we came to a tiny arroyo nestled down into a little gully. We were all out of breath. Eyes tortured.

"Okay, now git," Cody said.

"Cody, I—"

"Git I said! I don't want you a part of this."

I stood there. I felt like I had to stay, to own this, to say something for the burro. To be with him.

"Do what I'm tellin' ya," Cody said.

I stood for a second, my eyes locked with the man's. I looked one last time at Armendito, placed my hand on his neck, and then turned around and started walking. When I got back to the ranch some of the horses were still there in a line, staring.

The shot rang out.

There was no movement, nothing, just the sound of a gunshot in an empty land and my imagination. I stood and waited to see Cody walking toward the ranch, but he didn't come.

Then a second gunshot.

My eyes were tied to the trees waiting for Cody to emerge. I don't know how long it was, twenty minutes maybe. Then he came, head hanging. He was crying.

"Tell Tom I won't be good fer a while."

Cody jumped into his truck and sped out of the ranch. He was then drunk for two days straight.

I was tortured. The ending to Armendito's life. After all I had felt for all equines. We had failed in our responsibility to one of their kin.

It hurt.

As I struggled to look into the mirror after that I realized all I could do is be ready to know in the future, to have the knowledge and the feel for what is best to do for animals in my care, and to do everything I can for them.

And to always feel Armendito, with four legs strong, walking with me.

11 | Sun and Dust

THE DRIVE WE FEEL to follow a certain path will require a certain effort. When we pursue our passions and our dreams the tests and trials will line up in front of us. There's no avoiding it. And the big secret is only revealed once we live through it—that the tests and trials are what show us the way.

The paths a horse and human can take together are endless. There's dressage and reining; trail riding and jumping. Farm work and ranch work; groundwork and liberty work. There's tricks and games; and competitions and races. And then there's the work of caring for the horse, with his happiness being your greatest goal. Seeing a horse loving his horse life, out there in the field, relaxed and content.

Seems the most incredible journey can sometimes be incredibly simple.

We will be drawn to something. We may have known it from the beginning or maybe it became clear along the way. Maybe we want to ride in the Olympics or maybe we just love a quiet trail ride. Either way it will feel like a mission, and we will not be able to get away from it even if we try. We will either be doing it or thinking about doing it.

Within this we must always remember we are uniting with another living being that's on his own journey. Horses are individuals just like us, and they are drawn to certain things more than others. A horse that is curious and loves variety will love trail riding but will get bored and frustrated riding around in circles in an arena. A horse that's timid will feel safe in an arena but can become very scared out on the trail. We have to be sensitive to this. It's not all about us. We need to look for that great in-between where our journey and the horse's journey come together to create a third amazing journey. We must search for that middle land, riding in the arena to use a controlled setting to get better, working outside the arena to keep ourselves and our horses interested and inspired.

Most people are not training for the Olympics when they ride. But it becomes almost as big a deal with the pressure they put on themselves and their horses to learn certain things and advance to higher levels. How often do you see people smile or laugh when they ride? Often there is nothing but an intense look of concentration, the ride's worth decided by how well you and the horse performed. Let go of that. Have fun. Enjoy your horse and your life.

This is not to say we don't have to put in some hard work and that we shouldn't expect hard work from our horses—it's to say we should remember that riding should be fun. I have seen it time and time again: when people laugh, the horse shines.

When you and the horse have a common mission ahead of you, something wonderful happens: you aren't staring at each other anymore—you have something in front of you that you look at *together*. The spotlight is now on the path ahead. It might be a dressage test or three barrels. A versatility course or a herd of cattle. Going on a ten-mile trail ride or making your way over a jumper course. A lameness or a bad break-up. You and the horse are now a team, and together you look ahead, focused forward, working to find your way to a good day.

Friends helping each other through life.

And work and love become one and the same.

———

"What time is it, Roy?" asked Cody from where he was lying.

I opened my eyes and leaned up from the rock I was resting my head on. I had dozed off a little. Alto and Jake were standing ten feet away, each with one rein down to the ground. They both had sleepy eyes and one hind leg propped up in rest. Behind them ten horses grazed in a field.

Twelve Italian journalists were staying at the ranch. They were from different magazines in Italy, taking a tour of the American West. Our ranch was one of their stops. On the day they arrived Cody told Monica to have them all at the arena by two o'clock when we would bring in some horses.

We found a group and brought them in close to the ranch with time to spare. We let them graze while we rested a bit, our hats tipped over our eyes.

"It's almost two," I said.

"Alright. Let's give them Italians a show."

As we brought the horses running into the ranch the journalists scattered to find the perfect position for their camera shots. Cody pushed the horses toward the arena and Alto and I galloped ahead and opened the gate. After they were all in, I closed the gate as Cody ran around the ring with the horses. We then grabbed a couple saddles. The Italians ate it up. Cameras flashed and notes were taken and their eyes were locked on the show. Cody saddled a gray mare named Navajo. She was the biggest bucking horse on the ranch. As usual Cody liked to make sure the guests were pleased.

The second Cody asked Navajo to move out, her back arched and her head dropped to the ground and with loud grunting and snorting she wildly threw and twisted her body trying to lose the cowboy. She didn't.

Cody then told me to get on Tamayo, a bay gelding that could be a tough ride as well.

"Now git on and just ride like you ain't expectin' him to buck, but be ready fer anything," he said. "Remember what I told ya: get yer deep seat, keep yer mind in the middle of the saddle, and ride the ride."

It was going well until Tamayo let out a couple good size bucks I wasn't expecting, and I ended up straddling his neck. The bay helped me a bit though—he stopped and let me get my seat. I leaned my shoulders back and brought my feet forward and got deeper in the saddle. I rode on and smoothed out the rough and soon we were loping quietly around the arena together.

"Alright, cowboy," Cody said. "Let's doctor some cattle."

I had been working on my roping from horseback. Now it was for real.

We went into the cattle pen and Cody picked one out and calmly roped its horns. He dallied the rope to his saddle horn and pulled the line taught and waited for me to rope the cow's rear legs. Alto and I moved into place, settled, and I took my shot. Missed.

"Come on, Roy," said Cody. "Slow down, take yer time, and make it."

I recoiled my lariat and built another loop…took a couple swings, breathed, and steadied my hand…and let the loop fly. It landed perfectly, and the cow stepped into it and I drew the line tight and dallied to the horn. Cody and I then jumped down from the horses. I lay down with the cow and gently held her there while Cody gave her an injection of penicillin.

For the rest of the day the journalists followed us around taking pictures. They mostly photographed Cody, the classic cowboy. They got right up around him, snapping pictures while he was just standing there, casually talking to somebody. At times this seemed to anger Cody, something I hadn't seen in him yet.

After Armendito something in him had changed. He was a little harder, a little darker. What happened with Armendito had stirred up something inside him.

"Bully escaped sometime in the night," Cody said to me over breakfast. "I was thinkin' maybe you could ride out and lay eyes on where he's at."

Bully was the ranch bull. He was immense, weighing in at around three quarters of a ton with a horn span of four feet. We usually let him stay out, being he usually stayed near the ranch, but some of the local ranchers had asked that we keep him in because he had been bothering their herds.

"He likes to go hang out with Manolo's herd," Cody went on to say, "near the border fence, just west of Sasabe. Just go out and find him. It takes more than one rider to bring him in. I gotta stay and meet with a guy that may be takin' the third cowboy position."

The sun was just coming up. Some of the horses were still eating as the first morning rays warmed their backs. I walked out and met Alto and stood with him a while. He seemed happy. I led him to the hitching posts and saddled him. On one side of the saddle I tied my lariat. I considered tying the binoculars on the other side but didn't. Bully was big enough to see.

I got up on Alto and leaned back and scratched his hindquarters, then his withers. He turned his head back and nuzzled my boot. Every time I got on we did this now, like some sort of pre-flight check. *You're here and I'm here.*

We walked along a dry, sandy riverbed toward the border. We passed by the ranch graveyard and stopped. Scattered everywhere were the bones of horses and cattle and other farm animals. Whole and half sculls stared at us from the ground, half buried in the sand and dirt and brush that had grown up around them. Memories, alive and well, from the ranch's near three hundred years of history. Alto and I looked on, paying our respects, wondering about all the stories this sacred place held.

I rode out onto an open flat and there was the border fence. On the other side was Mexico. Another half hour of riding and we came to a hilltop and saw Manolo's herd and there he was. Easy to see. Twice the size of those around him. And he saw me. A man on a horse riding toward him—Bully knew what that meant. I took a deep breath and talked to Alto. He knew what this was too. He was a ranch horse who was good at this sort of thing long before I ever met him. He had taught me about it.

I thought about what Cody had said. What could it hurt though, just riding over there toward the bull?

I moved in a zigzag line trying to disguise my intentions and rode into the herd, moving amongst the cows like a polite gentleman who had come for a visit. One by one they all looked up at me. As I got closer, I saw Bully's eyes fixated on me, a line of drool blankly hanging from his mouth. I got as close to him as I thought I could and stopped Alto. There we were, the three of us, staring at each other. Alto's eyes never left him. The drool hung there. I looked away, like I was just enjoying the day.

But then I slowly turned my gaze back onto the bull, and it betrayed me.

Bully pulled back onto his haunches and turned and sprinted down the hill. He was as quick as a cat. Alto set back onto his haunches and prepared to give chase. I hesitated…then let him go. Within seconds we went from zero to sixty with Alto digging across the ground after the bull, fully committed. Bully came to a line of mesquite and without hesitation he crashed through it like a boulder. Tree and bush parted for the massive animal. Knowing the thorns and the thickness of the brush I eased Alto to a stop. Bully ran on, crashing through everything in his path. The noise of his movement fading away into the distance.

I sat there on Alto for a second. He waited for a decision. With a slight inflection from my seat, we started cantering along the line of trees looking for a way through. We finally came to a section where we could make it to the bottom of the hill. I knew Bully was probably miles away by now, but I took Alto up to a slow canter and we moved along the land, my eyes scanning from side to side for any sign.

I spent a good deal of time searching. I thought we had lost him. Cody knew the bull well and he was right, it couldn't be done by just one rider. *Oh well*, I thought, *it was fun to try...*

Standing in the shade of a tree was Bully. We startled him. His look said it all. *You're still here?* it said. A line of drool still dangling. *How did you find me?*

Alto danced his feet in anticipation.

Bully sat back on his haunches.

And we were off again. Crashing through bushes, zigging and zagging, the bull changed direction on a dime for no reason. It was like chasing a hummingbird. But this land was different, the trees more sparse, it was more open and Alto and I glided along at a gallop, cutting to the left and then to the right, keeping Bully in our sights, staying with him like a water skier in the wake of a speedboat.

And then I realized we were going in the direction of the ranch.

We can do this.

Bully seemed to realize that very same thing. Suddenly he cut back and tried to make it back past us. But Alto and I were of the same mind. Our gallop was a stop in no time. Bully ran back at us until only a tree was between us, a great big mesquite. He tried to get by us by running to the left of the tree, but we cut him off. He tried to go right, we cut him off.

It was here I felt something I had never felt before. If Bully wanted to get around me, he could. There was no way I could be quick enough in my riding to stay with him.

But Alto...that was a different story.

Alto took over and like he was trying to rival Bully's quickness, he dropped down into a cat-like stance and shadowed the old bull's movement, cutting him off at every try. I let go and trusted Alto and just followed Bully with my eyes. I sat deep in the saddle and moved with my horse.

The battle of quickness between horse and bull grew and grew until one cracked....

The bull gave up.

He turned and tried to run wide around us, but I saw that if we backtracked a little, we could come out ahead of him and cut him off. To Alto it must have looked like we were dropping off the chase, but he trusted where I was taking him. We came out and sprinted ahead. Bully turned back and started running toward the ranch again. Alto and I followed confidently, letting him know there was only one direction he could go.

The ranch came into view, and with that, another dilemma: *Okay, I got him here, now what do I do with him?*

Bully ran faster, Alto and I ran faster. I saw Cody and a tall man standing at the main corral area. They sprinted for the gate, hoping they could get there in time. People and horses and bulls all ran as hard as they could, and I didn't know how this was going to end.

Bully did though.

He ran for the corral fence and never stopped. He jumped higher than I was aware a bull could jump, which is why I guess he escaped so easily in the first place. The bull's leap took the top board with him. Alto and I came to a sliding stop at the fence behind him. In the center of the corral, Bully turned to face us, looking like he hoped we would finally leave him alone.

Cody walked up to Alto and me. "Looks like I missed quite a chase," he said.

"Yeah," I replied, out of breath.

"Didn't I tell ya not to be tryin' to bring him in on yer own?"

"Yeah," I admitted, not knowing what else to say. "Sorry."

He smiled like he was laughing to himself. "Well…today, at least, I'd say you earned the right to wear that hat."

I smiled. I laid my hand on Alto's neck and withers and I conveyed with all my heart how thankful I was, how in awe of him I was. His head turned and his eye looked back to me, and there it was, the feeling I would get. Something simple, something easy, something all the way right. Alto brought his nose around and nuzzled the tip of my boot.

I almost felt like going into that pen now and setting that bull free, tipping my chocolate-brown Stetson to him, and letting him go back to where he wanted to be.

The tall man's name was Arturo and he was hired on as the third cowboy at the Rancho de la Osa. He was thirty-two, from Arizona, the son of Mexican immigrants. He had been married but was now divorced and had a six-year-old son who lived with his ex-wife.

"You find I might be hard sometimes but I'm a straight-shooter." Cody said the familiar words to Arturo as we walked into the big corral. "We run a cowboy operation here and that's a lot of work. We work hard, but we play hard, and we have a lot of fun. Ain't that right, partner?"

"That's right," I said, with my own developing cowboy squint and nod.

"The place is beautiful," said Arturo with a slight Mexican accent. "Just what I'm looking for. A lot of the other ranches around here don't do the stuff you've talked about."

He was a big guy, pretty tall, and all muscle. He wore the dress of a cowboy—the big-heeled leather boots, the worn-out Wrangler jeans, big belt buckle, button-up long-sleeve shirt, and a white straw hat. We got along from the start. He had a friendly, honest way about him. He seemed genuinely happy to just be at the ranch.

That night after supper we went back to Cody's cabin and sat on the porch having beers and telling stories of the past places we had worked. Even though I didn't have much experience to draw upon, my rattlesnake and finger stories held the floor for a while. Arturo's grandfather had been a *vaquero*, a Mexican cowboy, and Arturo was now following in his footsteps. He held the cowboy way of life in high regard, like a religion almost, so he and Cody bonded immediately.

Cody got pretty drunk. He started to get emotional.

"Bein' a cowboy is more than a job. It's a way of life. In how you respect and treat those around ya, animal and human," he said, almost tearing up. "And it fills ya up! It's all ya need, the cowboy life. The land and the horses."

Cody looked away like he was hurting on the inside.

"It's all ya need," he repeated.

The three of us worked well together. The workload became more manageable and the work with the guests easier. Arturo shadowed me for a week and then started taking out the slow rides on his own. I took out most of the advanced rides, with Cody making a guest appearance every now and then.

It was a simple life of simple pleasures. Getting up at sunrise and taking care of the animals then heading in for breakfast and talking over the day's work. We'd then head out to the corrals and get the horses ready and go for the morning ride. Sometimes all three of us would ride, sometimes just one or two. The cowboys that didn't ride would get work done around the ranch, working with horses or fixing fences.

At the end of the day Cody, Arturo, and I would head back to one of our rooms and put on some country music and crack open the beers. This became our afternoon ritual. Since none of us had a refrigerator, we made sure to always have ice on hand from the kitchen, and this had the beers tasting better than any refrigerator could. There are beers in the Sonoran Desert, and then there are ice-cold beers in the Sonoran Desert.

Arturo would turn on his favorite country music, usually Chris LeDoux, and we would recap the day, the good and bad of it, the happiness within it all.

One afternoon Arturo dug through one of his duffle bags. He pulled out a pair of spurs. "Here," he said, handing them to me. "They're an old pair I don't use anymore. You should take them."

I put them on and tried them out. With each step, with each jingle, they grew on me. I knew it was a big deal, a cowboy giving another cowboy a pair of spurs.

One morning we all met out at the corrals at feeding time and the sun was just coming up. Arturo was driving the tractor while Cody and I stood in the trailer tossing hay. We were making our way around when Arturo pointed to the east.

It was the most beautiful sunrise I will ever see.

"Hey, look at ol' Cocoa!" said Cody with a smile.

Cocoa the Mustang was jumping and bucking, excited about feeding time, excited about life. The energy passed on to some of the other horses and they took to having some fun too.

"Yeeehaaaaa!" yelled Arturo as he waved his hat over his head.

Being a part of a morning like that was what life was all about for us.

One day Arturo and I were out gathering horses together. We went to the usual spots and had good luck, coming across eight early on, and decided to get those horses back to the ranch. The group went soft and easy with no running. As we went, we spotted four more in the distance. We decided I would ride out after them and see if I could get them started toward the ranch, and we would then meet up with the two groups at the watering hole.

Alto and I went off at a canter and came to the ridge where we had seen the horses. They were still there, and I got them moving toward the watering hole. All went to plan. Arturo walked up with the other horses at the same time I got there. We let them get a drink and a few splashed and played in the water.

On the way home we came across three more horses. We slid them into the group, making the count fifteen. With that many in front of us we now had some work to do just to keep them together. Then we came to that mesquite forest.

All went well at first. But our constant moving up and down the line to keep them together got the energy up a little, and just when we thought we would be able to do the whole ride home at a walk, they took off. We weren't quite prepared and had to play catchup. We kept the herd together for a while but then they started spilling all over the place. We tried to keep our eyes on where they were ending up, but we lost them all…and soon we even lost each other. I didn't know where Arturo was, and that pretty surely meant he didn't know where I was either.

Alto and I rode around looking for anything with four legs. There was a lot of dust in the air, a lot of tracks going in every direction, and a lot of silence. I yelled for Arturo every thirty seconds or so and eventually we found each other. We went to tracking the horses as best we could, neither one of us wanting to tell Cody we lost that many. At last, we started coming to little groups—two here, four there. We went to work rebuilding our herd. It was hard going, riding in the middle of the mesquite, but we got them all back together and moving again.

Along the way we came to another horse with our brand, but I didn't recognize him. A tall, dark bay gelding that was limping. It bothered me that he was hurt and alone.

"We're getting him in," I said. "No matter how slow we have to go or if we lose the others."

Arturo agreed.

We now had to move slowly. One of us would have to ride up and stop the lead horse now and then so the big bay could keep up. The horses seemed to know exactly what was going on. They stopped and looked back at the bay and waited for him to catch up. Then on our signal the horses all continued on.

The gelding limped along. The look in his eye said he was trying his hardest.

"Let's take a break for a while," I said when he started to labor too much.

We came across another five horses grazing within a mile of the ranch.

We worked them into the herd and our number was now twenty-one. There was a lot of work to be done in keeping them directed the right way, keeping horses from breaking off, and keeping the herd at a speed the lame horse could travel.

"So, what's your story?" Arturo asked while we rode. "Why are you here?"

"I needed to be around horses and needed to be paid for it," I said. "How 'bout you?"

"Me? Well, my grandfather was a cowboy. One of the great vaqueros of these borderlands. So I've always known the life. The simple pleasures, the contentment. That sounded awful good to me after living through some… hard times."

"Oh yeah?" I said, giving him a chance to continue if he wanted.

"I spent some time in prison. I got caught up in a drug thing I wasn't supposed to be a part of. A friend was doing the deal and he wanted me to come. He was going to pay me, so… so I did it. I needed the money."

"How long were you in for?"

"A year. I then got a job on a dude ranch in Arkansas, then this one. Don't talk much with my ex-wife and I don't get to see much of my son now 'cause of what happened. One mistake, you know?"

We rode a while before Arturo spoke again. "I guess that's why I'm here now. The horses don't care about any of that."

We rode into the ranch proudly with the twenty-one horses. I thought about what Cody had said about rushing. I thought about it in my own life, in my interactions with the horses, in my everyday rituals. I was rushing a lot. Without even noticing it.

I wondered how many things I had missed because of it.

———————

A week later Cody put on a three-day horse-starting clinic for the guests. As he worked with the horse, a young mare, I focused on two things—where he was coming from on his inside (attitude) and where he was coming from on the outside (technique). It started to click with me. First you had to come from a very balanced place on the inside. Good intentions for the horse and a relaxed confidence in what you were doing. In the technique, the first step was getting the horse's complete attention. It was what every teacher first asked the students for, but it seemed few horse people asked for it from their horses and many weren't even aware of where their horse's attention was in the first place. When the horse isn't paying attention, of course he won't do well with whatever we are asking him to do.

After that Cody worked on making sure the mare saw him as leader and that he had her best try. And you could see in the horse's eyes and ears when she was paying attention and trying her hardest. From there she started to relax more and sights and sounds that bothered her in the beginning faded away. You could see her feeding off Cody's grounded and confident energy. What pulled it all together was his love for what he was doing. You could see Cody's love for the mare.

I thought of how we mess it up. Not having a mutual respect and the horse not seeing us fully as leader. Not having confidence and not knowing what to do and getting frustrated and then blaming the horse. Rushing. Being rough with the horse. Working with a horse that is not a good match for us. And then I thought, *It's all in how we approach it. The horse is already perfect.*

That afternoon we went back to Arturo's room as usual. Cody told stories of his days as a "bullfighter"—what people commonly call "rodeo clowns." At one point Arturo shot up in his chair.

"Oh my God, I thought I knew you!" he said. "You were signing autographs at a rodeo in Prescott. It would have been around five years ago, and I was there with my son and we got your autograph!"

Cody didn't seem surprised at this. "Yeah, I was probably there," he said.

"Used to come through Prescott quite a bit." He seemed like he didn't want to talk about it.

Arturo put on his Chris LeDoux *Live* album. The sun had long since gone down. We drank and talked and listened to the music. *He's still out there riding fences, still makes his living with his rope.* We all got drunk. Arturo sang along with the music, badly, but the heart he sang with made up for it. *He's a knight in leather armor, still living by the code.* The music chanted the cowboy way of life. *The last to quit, the first to buy the beer…*

I looked over at Cody. "I get it now," I said.

He looked back at me with a heavy amount of feeling to his eyes, they glistened a bit.

"You get it now?"

I nodded, not taking my eyes off his.

"You got the heart. You got the potential. You know horses like you knew 'em before you knew 'em. You still got a lot to learn…but yer on yer path."

I felt it. The greatness of it all and the sadness of it all. *He never drew a breath that wasn't free…*

We kept drinking. Cody sat on Arturo's bed. I sat in a chair in the corner beside the cooler. "Pass me another, Cowboy." I heard every fifteen minutes or so. Our boots, all with spurs strapped on, sat at various spots on the floor. The windows were open, the desert sounds outside. Cody went silent for a while. Then he passed out. His body swayed a bit and he fell to the floor. Arturo and I leapt to try and stop the fall but it was useless. His body was dead weight, dead drunk. I picked up his head and tried to wake him but he was done. It was the sleep of a man who had passed out like that many times before.

"Let him lie there," said Arturo.

We sat back down but neither of us could keep our eyes off Cody, passed out on the floor.

"I knew that I knew him from somewhere," said Arturo.

There was something heavy in the air as we talked about the man.

"That's what happens," Arturo then said with a presence of wisdom about him. "That's what happens to old cowboys."

He didn't sound sad. He sounded like he had seen it before, and it was normal.

We let Cody sleep where he fell. He woke us up at five the next morning for feeding.

Some days later all the guests decided to go to Nogales for the day. They wanted Cody to go with them, and after Arturo and I assured him over and over the place would be okay without him, he gave in and went. Something in him had seemed to be building up, getting ready to pop, and it seemed like a good idea if he took a day off.

We spent the afternoon cleaning the corrals. We laughed, we joked. I made up a love song in the limited Spanish I knew and with some terms Arturo taught me.

"This is what it should be like," said Arturo. "Getting the work done and having fun doing it."

We finished mucking the corrals and then got the fence work done like we told Cody we would. I was back in my room getting ready to open the cantina when he came back. His boots stormed across the paved walkway. A quick and powerful three-beat knock hit my door. I opened it and there he was, red-faced.

"The corrals look good but what about the fence!" He was drunk.

"What do you mean?"

"You know what I'm talking about! The fence, it's only half done!"

He had a glazed-over stare like his eyeballs were sweating from the booze and anger. His body had a sway to it. Everything about him reeked of out-of-control.

"Cody, I don't know what you're talking about," I said calmly. "We cleaned out all of the corrals and we took care of that length of fence like you asked us to."

"Bull! I put you in charge and half the fence still ain't done!"

I saw the future. I would say I was sorry, say I would try harder, do better. I would run right out there and continue working on whatever he was talking about, him telling me that was a cowboy's way, me praising him for the learning experience.

But it just didn't feel right. Not this time.

"Cody, if you want to talk about this we can, but not like this. I mean, as far as we knew, we got all the work done."

"You think today was a day off for ya 'cause I was gone, do ya?"

"No, just take it easy."

"No! We're gonna talk about this now! You wanna get fired?"

"What? No, I just don't want to talk to you like this."

"Fine then, you're fired!"

I looked at him and shook my head. I couldn't deal with it. There was a loss of mutual respect here. I walked past him and across the courtyard without looking back.

"You're fired!" he yelled again.

I got the cantina ready for the guests. Lydia the office manager came in and I talked with her. She told me Cody sometimes got like this.

I watched from the cantina as Cody stormed out of Arturo's room and walked fast across the ranch. Minutes later Arturo came into the cantina.

"I just got fired," he said.

"Me too," I replied.

"He came into my room screaming that we didn't finish the fence work today, but I thought we did," said Arturo, not comprehending it.

Cody came up to the doorway of the cantina and looked right at me. "I need to talk with you out here," he said.

I went outside.

"Now listen to me," he said. "I'm a straight-shooter and I tell it like it is. I'm hard on ya but it's for yer own good. I don't wanna fire ya. But you gotta get the work done."

"Cody, you told us we didn't have to finish all the corrals, but we did and you told us to just fix that one side of the fence and we did. We thought we'd done *more* than you asked."

He still had that glazed look to his eyes. His soul was twisted and sweating and out of breath. "You think you can work until supper," he started, "and then just punch out because it's supper time? Boy, that ain't what this life is about. You think you know what this life is about?"

"If you don't think I can handle it, fine. I came here to work with horses and to do the best job I can with the guests. That's it. And now you're firing everybody, I guess."

"Arturo can't keep up when we bring in horses, and he's got his own ways that don't work around here."

"Oh, come on, Cody! Stop talking about him to me and about me to him behind our backs!"

"Don't tell me how to talk! I'll say what I gotta say! You think you know horses? Let me tell you something, boy, in the horse's eye, secrets shatter and lies die!"

"Whatever. I'm done." I started to move past him, but he got in my way.

"You're fired!"

"Yeah, I know, I heard that already," I said as I tried again to walk by. He stepped in front of me once more, wouldn't let me pass. I looked him in the eye and saw he was taking his craziness to a new level.

We were about to fight. And I was okay with it.

How did it come to this? I love this guy.

Arturo came out of the cantina, and at first I thought it was to break up anything that started, then I realized it was to back me up. Lydia moved between Cody and me.

"Come on, guys, stop this! Cody, go away!" she said.

Cody stepped back and looked away from me. He swiped his dirty white Stetson off his head and ran his hand through his sweaty hair. He then looked to the ground like he was shamed.

"I'm just tryin' to teach 'em what they gotta know," he said. He wouldn't look anyone in the eye now. He turned and walked away.

I watched him go, his silhouette fading more into the darkness until it was gone.

———————————

It was six in the morning. I looked at myself in the mirror. My beard was long, straggly. My face dry and leathery. My eyes tired, older.

Arturo and I met and went to feed. It was a cold morning, and the tractor wouldn't start. Nothing new. I choked it and waited a few seconds.

We heard it coming, the loud engine of Cody's truck. He came down through the ranch and pulled up beside us. He got out and walked over, his eyes never leaving the ground. No Stetson now, just a baseball cap.

"Tractor gets hard to start on these cold mornings," he said humbly. "Use the choke, let it warm up a little."

"Sure," I said.

"I'm leaving the ranch," he said.

"You're gonna leave?"

"Yeah, I'm leaving," he said softly. "I'm so wound up I don't know what I'm doing anymore. I messed up last night. Real bad. I messed up with you guys and I messed up with Tom and Monica."

Cody had spent the night knocking on Tom and Monica's door demanding to talk to them. Tom was gone to Tucson for the night and Monica was there alone. Cody knocked all night and had scared Monica to the point she didn't want to open the door.

"I'm real sorry for any trouble I've caused you boys," he said, looking me in the eye, waiting for an answer.

I looked at him straight and nodded slightly. "Where are you going to go?"

"Oh, I don't know. I'll be in touch. Maybe see ya again sometime."

He smiled and turned to walk away.

"Cody, wait," I said.

"It doesn't have to be this way, Cody," said Arturo.

"It does for me," replied Cody over his shoulder as he walked.

He got into his truck and drove out of the ranch.

I felt a world of gratitude toward Cody for what he had taught me. He was the most amazing horseman I had ever seen, and I thought of him as a friend. There was an inner balance to him, a love for land and animal and life. But with people he was sometimes short, hard. One day you could love him, the next hate him.

I didn't want the Cody I loved to go.

For the next week the ranch operation ran smoothly for the most part. We had a couple of families and a guy traveling by himself, John. He was forty-seven and his doctor had told him he was slowly going blind. He decided it was time to travel the world and do all the things he had always wanted to do. Riding a horse was on that list.

I ended up working a lot with a nine-year-old girl named Katie. She was with her family, and when it came to the horses, she wanted no part of them. Her parents convinced her to try riding, and I matched her with Kola, my go-to when I needed a horse that would take great care of a young or fearful guest. He became Katie's horse for the whole week and by the time her family had to leave, she was hugging him with tears in her eyes.

The ranch wasn't near the same though. It was missing a large chunk of its heart.

Arturo and I were unsaddling horses when Cody came around the corner of the tack room. He had on sneakers and the baseball hat. He walked slowly, hands in pockets, eyes to the ground.

"If you boys got a moment I'd like to talk with ya," he said.

Cody sat down on a crate, Arturo on the bench. I leaned up against the railing and eye contact was nowhere to be found.

"I'm sorry for anything I said or did that other night," Cody started. "I hope ya know I didn't mean anything by it."

Arturo and I nodded.

"You boys are a couple of great fellas. Top hands, both of ya. I was just wound up sa' tight I…I ain't never run a dude ranch before and I…well I don't wanna make excuses. The fact of the matter is I was wrong, and I apologize. That and I know I need to fix some things about myself. You see there's some things from my past that…sometimes they churn up inside a me and…"

He paused. It seemed he wanted to say so much but didn't know how to do it. He combined the miles and miles of what he wanted to say into the most simple statement he could muster.

"I need help," he said with sincerity.

This opened me up.

"I've had a good time here with you guys and I'd really appreciate the chance to come back. I've talked with Tom and Monica, and they say it's okay so long as I quit the drinkin' on the ranch. But it's you fellas and what you think that's important to me."

Cody looked at me to speak my mind on it.

"I just came here to work with the horses, Cody," I said.

"I know that's what you came here for," he said.

Cody's eyes were easy as he looked to me. They held truth. The man's heart was being laid out.

"Listen," I started, "I've made a lot of mistakes too, before here and while I've been working here. I know you've put up with a lot, with me learning and stuff. I just think it can be easier, without all the tension and all."

"I agree. It could be a lot more relaxed, couldn't it?" he said.

"The job is pretty fun if we all just let it be," said Arturo.

Cody smiled. He started shaking his head and his smile got bigger and bigger. "It is the best dang job in the world, ain't it?"

Cody, Arturo, and I all smiled in agreement. At some point my mind went to the horses. I thought about them and what they would think.

They all really liked Cody.

And so the three of us went back to work together. Cody stayed faithful to his new rule of not drinking on the ranch. He just had the guests going up to the Sasabe bar all the time now. It would get crazy. Away from the ranch it seemed there were no rules. Beers were popped open so quick it was as if people just liked the sound of it. People danced on the bar and outside we had roping contests with bar stools. I was almost getting good enough to beat Cody (when he was off and missed one). One by one we all let out a joyous yell, each one specific to the yeller, a cowboy yell exclaiming that *life is great at this moment.*

One night, Cody put his arms around Arturo and me as suds streamed down the sides of his chin. "Here's to the two best damn hands a guy could ever wanna work with!"

When the alarm clock screamed out the next morning it hurt real bad. I got myself together and pulled my boots on. My head pounded and the room twisted and turned. My hair hurt. I stumbled toward the door while buckling my pants.

Out in the corrals Arturo drove the tractor while Cody and I stood in the wagon and threw hay. The sun came up and set fire to the land and sky and the horses were excited and we hooted and hollered and laughed. Sun and horse and man came alive. I smiled and smiled, for the feeling of being up at that moment, a part of this great life.

So it was good again. Until Arturo was asked by Tom and Monica about his past.

Another Arizona dude rancher knew Arturo and had told them about what had happened. Tom and Monica asked why he hadn't told them, especially when questions about a possible employee's criminal record were part of the hiring process. He said he had avoided telling them out of concern he would not get the job.

I spoke to Tom and Monica on his behalf. "I've known Arturo to be a hard-working, honest man. He's good with the guests, he's a good cowboy, and he's a good friend."

It was good enough for Tom and Monica but not for Arturo. He was let down. Then it turned to frustration. He was proud and didn't want to be judged by his past. He went to talk to Tom and Monica again. It didn't go well and ended with him giving his notice.

"I know my past is gonna follow me," he told me. "I thought I could get beyond it, but maybe it won't be so easy."

I had become close with Arturo. Working the horses and the land the way we were it was impossible not to. "Why not stay?" I asked. "Just keep working. It will get better. I'm sure of it."

"No. I can get paid more at a local feed store back home where my parents live. I'll start new there."

He was set on leaving. I helped him pack his gear into his truck.

"You can keep those spurs I gave you," he said.

"Naw, you—"

"I want you to keep them."

I looked down at them on my boots. They fit perfectly. "Thanks, Arturo. I'll use them with honor."

"If they are on your boots, my friend, they could not be used otherwise."

We both looked around the ranch. The moment needed a pause in conversation.

"It's been a lot of fun working with you, cowboy," he said.

"We had some good rides," I replied.

"Yeah. We did."

We shook hands.

"Maybe someday we'll ride together again somewhere, huh?" he said.

"I hope so."

He got into his truck and drove away. I never saw Arturo again.

12 | A Home Within

WHEN I RUN through the fields with a horse, beside him or on his back, and there is nothing but freedom in front of us, between us, and within us…I feel the beauty of what we share together. I have found something inside myself in how I live life and in my feel for horses, and the horse has found something within himself and how he lives life and in his feel for me. It is between us now, a connection built upon our time together; all the joys and challenges, all the laughing and crying. The deeper the connection, the brighter the contentment within our shared movement.

As our journey with a horse grows and hours turn to days, days turn to years, and years turn to lifetimes, we find we need less to guide him. Something else has taken over. A grand knowing of each other. A far-reaching harmony. We communicate in ways unseen and not of this world alone. The heart speaking louder than any metal bit's pressure; the dedication to each other rising stronger than any whip or spur could inspire. The bond takes over for the halter and bridle and we travel as one, united in the feel for each other.

Horses are big, but they do not know they are big. They live by presence, feel, and energy. And when we have all their presence, feel, and energy choosing us and seeking our guidance, we are able to guide them from the slightest touch and softest movement, from the slightest and softest of thoughts. Halter and lead rope and bit and bridle are needed to assist us, they are our crutches. We need them to help us, not the horse, and for our safety and the horse's safety we use them. But as our ability strengthens and our connection deepens so should the amount and severity of our equipment lessen. We use it until we feel ready to cast it off, arriving back where we began, looking at a free horse standing there in front of us.

What they do with that freedom is all their own. If we have been working with their minds and spirits and not just their bodies, then maybe they stay, for bonds born deep within do not leave when equipment leaves. So maybe the horses stay. And maybe what we thought working with horses was all about, maybe we see it differently now. Maybe it's not about *training* horses. Maybe it's about something much more grand, and much more simple. Much more meaningful. Maybe it's about our hearts.

Maybe that's all everything ever is about.

I looked into the mirror. The beard was much longer. There were lines all over my face. My skin was weathered, worn. My eyes...

It was back to the way it had started: Cody and I running around the Sonoran Desert. There had been a lot of stressful times on the ranch in the last months but somehow when it got back to just the two of us, we settled down and went to work like we had been running the ranch for years. We had a mutual respect. And we both saw horses as our saving grace.

"Free up those hindquarters, Roy," he said to me as I was riding a horse in our arena. "That's your gateway to helping the horse to bend well and have good flexibility. Keeping those hindquarters soft and supple will give you the control you need in tight times as well as the foundation to get the shoulders and ribcage soft. It also helps the horse to breathe, stretching through that body of his."

I worked on my riding a lot, riding as many horses as I could. Each horse had his own feel—and the more horses I could feel the better my feel would be for horses. I first tried to get an idea of who the horse was as an individual—was he confident or timid, stoic or playful—and then I worked with them from that point of view. I spent a lot of time trying to get a better feel for my groundwork. I spent days working with horse after horse, loose in the round pen. I set up a video camera to record myself and then watched the film in the evening, figuring out what I could do better to help the horse understand where I was coming from.

We had a ranch rodeo. We did cattle cutting, barrel racing, and the pony express relay race. I was the anchor for my team, and we were behind. My teammate raced to me and handed me the pony express bag, and Alto and I took off and sprinted down to the other end of the arena where Cody was holding the new horse I would have to get on and ride, Cocoa the Mustang. I jumped off Alto while he was still running, handed him to Cody, grabbed the horn on the saddle Cocoa was wearing and sprung up onto his back without touching a stirrup and took off into a gallop. People cheered. I asked Cocoa for all he had and he gave it, digging for every step. As we crossed the finish line, I knew we had won. I pulled up on the reins, but instead of stopping, Cocoa turned hard to the left, still at a gallop. I lost balance. The harder I tried to pull him to a stop with my one hand on the reins the more he veered left at a gallop and the arena fence was suddenly in front of us. I dropped the sack I was holding in my right hand and instantly saw why Cocoa was running left—I had been riding with an extra foot of slack in the right rein, rendering it ineffective, something I didn't see because of the sack I was holding.

And now it was too late. Cocoa and I came up to the fence at a dead run. Whether he was going to stop, go through it, or over it was out of my hands now.

He came to a sliding stop and reared as high as horses go. I tried to lean forward and give him slack in the reins as best I could, but I fell off and landed hard on the ground on my back, staring straight up. Through the massive uproar of dust I could see movement. It was the Mustang's front hooves. Cocoa was still rearing up, now spinning on his hind legs and striking out at the air to regain balance. And those hooves started to fall. They needed to land.

I covered my head and closed my eyes as the hooves came down.

I opened my eyes. To each side of my head was a hoof. Cocoa danced over me and moved away, not even brushing my body with his feet. Then I heard Cody's hurried voice. "You okay?" The look in his eye told me how bad the fall had been.

I calmly stood up out of the dirt, picked up my hat, dusted it off, put it back on and went to catch Cocoa like I had planned it all. This was my first fall from a horse. As people watched me walk to Cocoa I felt…embarrassed.

Why? Why would I feel embarrassed? Surfers and skiers wipe out, mountain bikers fall. Why would someone feel embarrassed about falling off a horse?

I felt the eyes watching me as all stayed quiet like they were waiting for me to say something. I looked up at Alto where Cody had left him ground tied. He was looking at me with a wide eye as he followed my walk across the arena.

That night Cody came to see me in my room. "Boy, that was a hell of a ride you put on ol' Cocoa today," he said with a smile.

"Yeah. Too bad I didn't finish it."

"You still feeling alright are ya?"

"It feels like everything is still where it's supposed to be."

Cody nodded. He cared. "You know why people get hurt with horses, don'tcha?" he asked. "It's 'cause horses are so big."

I laughed.

"No, seriously. Horses are the kindest animals in the world. Just when they're scared at something or frustrated with ya, they jump around a bit.

It's hard to keep yer head sometimes…mentally and literally."

"I don't know," I said. "That was my first fall and I feel stupid. I was rushing and I didn't feel the slack in that right rein."

Cody looked down at the floor and started nodding. "Well, there's an ol' Mexican saying," he said as he looked back up to me. "It ain't enough for a man to learn how to ride, he must also learn to fall."

I looked into Cody's eyes, realizing I already knew what he was about to tell me.

"What I'm sayin' is," he started, "is there ain't nothin' wrong with fallin' so long as yer heart and yer head were in the right place before it happened, and after it happened. Were yours?"

I laughed.

"Answer me, were they?"

"Yeah," I said.

"Alright then. So don't bond yerself to what's past. Let what happened learn ya to have a better feel for the horses the next time. It's okay to fall if just so as to learn how to get back up. Make sense?"

"Yeah. I get ya."

"Alright then."

Cody went to the door. As he was leaving he turned to me. "There's always a moment, Roy," he said.

"A moment?"

"A feeling. A sign. Nothing happens out of the blue. It could be how you felt going into it, it could be one second before it happens…but there's always a moment. And it gives you a choice. There's always a choice. In everything."

He stood there in silence. "I'll see you in the mornin'," he then said and walked out and closed the old wooden door behind him.

The next day we had to freeze-brand cattle. They were getting mixed in with other herds around Sasabe and we needed to be able to tell them apart. Cody and I started out roping the calves from horseback. I worked hard on what Cody had showed me, how to rope them lightly and to not pull them or hurt them in any way. Cody would then dismount and lead the guests in the branding process.

We then moved to the full-grown longhorns. We set it up so we had four guests riding and separating the cattle, and six guests as the ground team. Either Cody or I would be riding while the other was on the ground for support. Cody usually stayed on the ground since he could direct things better there. The riders would separate the target cow from the herd and push the cow into a small chute connected to the arena made for the purpose of branding and doctoring cattle.

The guests were getting to be real cowboys. Not for fun but because we had a job to do, and you had to fill in where needed. We would herd a cow in and I would jump down off of Alto to help get ropes on her. The longhorns were big and strong and unpredictable. The ropes could be your friends or enemies depending on your awareness. The people on horseback had to be there at the ready but working on the ground was the more dangerous part. Horns and hooves were sometimes flying. Following Cody's lead, I knew there could be no hesitation, you just had to dive in there and do what needed to be done.

With the dust and sweat on our faces and the bumps and bruises on our bodies we all walked directly to the cantina after the branding.

The next day Cody hooked up our two draft horses, Brando and Luna, to the big wagon. We threw some hay bales in for something to sit on, stocked a cooler full of beer, and just around sunset we took the guests for a tour of the land. I rode as outrider on Alto. The border patrol sometimes flew down the dirt roads, so I stayed a little ahead of the wagon to make sure nothing was coming around the corners.

Riding with Alto at sunset with some good people. It seemed it was all my life needed.

When the day came for this batch of guests to leave some of them cried. They had become amazingly tight in their time at the ranch. We opened up the cantina for a few tequila shots before everybody had to go. I thought about how they were heading back to a different world, far away in a land I had not seen for a long time.

I thought about my life. It was pretty simple in a good way. I knew the horses and they knew me. I knew my life and it knew me with nothing hidden, nothing misunderstood.

I was in danger. I was in danger of not going back. I felt like I could get up in this land every morning and ride a horse every day for the rest of my life. And love it.

It felt like home.

I decided to teach myself bareback riding during my lunch breaks. I got up on Alto but quickly found out he was too narrow for someone to learn on. I walked into the corral and looked at the different horses. I chose a nice sorrel gelding named HR because he was kind of beefy and pretty steady.

It felt good. It was the same feeling I had that first time I rode without a bridle. Really *feeling* the horse. Freedom. Walking felt good so I decided to trot.

It became pretty clear there was only one way to ride a horse bareback. You either ride the right way or you fall off. There is no in-between. You can't ride *poorly* or ride *okay*. There were no styles—no hunt seat, Western seat, dressage seat. You had to have the proper balance and feel to ride a horse, or you were on the ground. Once you started to lose it, even by just a bit, you were pretty much either clinging to the horse's neck or falling.

I went at it with an understanding of how much focus it would take. I was proactive, keeping my seat deeper in the direction I was traveling.

Pretty soon I was trotting figure eights. Cantering soon after that. By the end of the week, it was going so well I was inspired to try something.

HR and I were in sync, we had a rhythm in our riding, in it together. It felt right—without wanting it to or needing it to—and the opportunity for something more seemed to find its way to us.

We rode bareback *and* bridleless, cantering around in circles amongst the other horses in the corral. His movement was different. His eyes were different. The wind in my face felt different. The freedom of mind, body, and spirit.

I slid off HR's back and hugged him around his neck. He looked back at me, and I rubbed his forehead vigorously. He looked at me like it was a great moment, something that he had never felt before either. Like it was just as thrilling and satisfying to him.

Horses know what is going on, I thought.

It was late fall and the early mornings became cold enough that you had to respect them with coats until the sun came up.

Every step I walked was punctuated by the soft jingle of spurs. It became a part of me and my movement. The sound they made was specific to me and me alone. When I rode Alto, or any of the other horses, I never had to use them. But I still wore the spurs for how they made me feel. They filled in for me in some way, giving me a storied place in the world, connecting me to a lineage. It seemed connecting yourself to something revered could relax the need for belonging.

I would think about them, though, the spurs. Metal with some sort of round or blunted or pointed ends, designed to apply pressure to a horse's belly. A cue he would move forward from in the hopes of not feeling that pressure any more. *What does that feel like—having the thought that spurs could touch, press, or jab into your belly?* I didn't think I would like it. Even if I know the person wouldn't use them, I would still know they were there.

When I rode Alto, a shift of my eyes or seat or just my voice was all we needed. It didn't feel like he was just looking for a release of pressure. He was teaching me to ride, that horse. Giving me something deep in the form of an education I was only partly aware of.

With the guests Cody was talkative, joking, charming, and charismatic. His old self. But on the inside, something still ate away at him. We had always talked while we rode together, but lately we would ride for hours without saying a word.

One day we were out looking for horses. We had both been quiet for a while. Suddenly he broke the silence like he wanted to say something that had been on his mind for a long time.

"You see, there was a woman I once knew."

I turned to look at him as we rode side by side.

"And we were in love, I guess. I sure did love her. She seemed to feel the same. It was…as real as it gets, I think. Heck I never expected it or even looked for it, but we got pritty tight. Changes everything. Everything ya thought ya knew, everything ya thought ya wanted. It just…turns everything upside down. In a good way. When I was in it, boy, I loved every second of it. Made ya really want to get up in the mornin' ya know? Made ya wanna make something of yerself. Do it right."

The way he was telling me this, the look in his eyes.

"She was a city girl though. Didn't like it much in the wide-open land. Wanted me to come with her. Illinois. Said I could get a job at a horse barn in the suburbs as an instructor or something, that they would love me there. So I went." He started to shake his head ever so slowly, remembering the time and the place.

"But it didn't take," he said.

We rode for a while before he spoke again. He turned to look at me from Jake's back as he did. "When you're runnin', sooner or later you gotta make a choice, Roy. Are you runnin' *from* something...or runnin' *to* something."

We had to check the cattle for infection since we had recently branded them. Cody and I were on horseback, Jose and Hector supported us from the ground. Cody was running with Jake alongside a fence, chasing a cow that wasn't more than five yards ahead of him. The cow turned hard to the inside and Cody and Jake stayed right with them. Cody had a loop twirling above his head.

There was a patch of cement in this pen about ten feet by ten feet. I have no idea what it was originally put there for. It was usually covered by dirt.

Jake's hooves slid right out from under him. He slammed down onto his side with Cody still in the saddle. It was a violently hard fall and dust exploded into the air where they were last seen like it was a magician's trick making them disappear. But when the dust cleared, they were flat on the ground, horse and human, both with sharp, stunned looks.

I rode up and got down and the first thing I saw was Cody's eyes as he looked up at me.

It had nothing to do with the fall. It had to do with his life. He looked tired from the fight that had been going on inside of him. He lay there and looked at me like I knew exactly what he was thinking right then, like I had been witness to his whole existence. Like I knew his fate as well as he did.

On this morning, at that moment, he felt beaten. I saw it in his heart.

Cody stood up. Jake stood up. They were both shaken but appeared to be okay. Cody was bleeding here and there, and he couldn't move one of his hands well. Something was clearly wrong with it but there being no immediate doctor within two hours, he just went back to work.

"You'll be home for Christmas though, right?" Mom asked.

"I don't know," I said.

Silence from her end of the phone.

Late one night we were in the cantina, a fire going, with two women named Grace and Harper.

"Most people would give anything to live the life you guys have," said Grace.

"Most people have no idea what this life is like," replied Cody.

"What are you saying?" Harper said quickly. "You don't love what you do? You're cowboys. Everybody loves you guys. You have one of the coolest jobs in the world."

"I love my life. No question," said Cody. "I love every moment I'm in the saddle, every moment I'm with a horse. It ain't a choice for me, it's in me and I gotta do it or I ain't right. But it takes away from…other things in life you might want. And that can take a lot outta ya."

"What can be so bad about being a cowboy?" asked Grace.

"Loneliness. Regret. Resentment," I said as I looked directly at Cody.

The women turned to look at me.

Cody chuckled and pushed his Stetson back. "So, you're learnin', huh, Roy?" he said. "Why then are you still here?"

I looked down at my beer. "Cause it's where I'm supposed to be right now."

"Just right now?" asked Harper.

"There was something missing in me for the first part of my life. Here, I feel…"

"Complete?" said Grace.

I thought for a moment. I thought about those first horses I saw on the night of the talk with Ally. What I saw in their eyes that night. *They didn't want to be anything more than they were.*

Cody watched me, waiting intently on my answer.

"Complete... incomplete..." I started. "What does it ever mean? They're just labels we put on ourselves when really it's all about whether we're happy or not. If we are following our passions and our loves and our dreams. If we're being ourselves. If we love our lives."

"So...do you love your life?" said Harper.

"I'm learning something," I said. "Or discovering it, maybe. That looking to be made whole by somebody or something, that thinking it's up to the world to save you, and that the world is out of your control…well, there's always a choice in there, somewhere. A choice to stay where you are or go forward. Every day. Every moment."

Cody smiled ever so slightly from underneath his hat.

The next day I was riding with some guests, and we spotted Bully a couple miles from the ranch. He had once again been missing for a while. We rode back to the ranch and met Cody and the group he had as they were dismounting.

"Cody," I said excitedly. "We found Bully."

Cody was quickly back up on Jake. "Alright," he said. "Anybody that wants to come, let's go. But be ready. This ain't gonna be no bumpety-bump ride."

People blankly looked around at each other and then the brave ones began to get back up on their horses. They all knew we had been looking for Bully and had heard how big he was. Some guests who decided to go said goodbye to their loved ones like they were going off to war.

We rode out, ten in all. As soon as we were through the ranch gate Cody took Jake up into a lope and everybody followed. We saw where Bully was, resting in the middle of some thick brush that left little room for horse and rider to get through.

I rode up beside Cody. "How you wanna do this?" I asked.

Cody started riding down toward the bull. "Send two down with me. Tell the others to get north of him and push him toward the ranch if he gets by us."

Before I could talk to him about it, he was gone. I could see it in his eyes. He was a little out of control right now.

"Okay," I yelled as I turned toward the guests. "Carl and Elizabeth go with Cody. The rest of you move around the bull that way and form a line as best you can."

The guests followed my directions. But before they were in place Cody started to push Bully. Guests started to ask what to do. Cody didn't answer.

I gave directions as best I could. "Just fall in behind him!" I yelled. "And stay out to the sides of him, keep the bull pointed toward the ranch!"

But before everyone could get set the action started. Bully, as he always did when he saw us, went running. Cody and Jake sprinted after him. Without knowing what else to do the guests started running their horses as well, either trying to help or just keep up. As usual the bull made quite a run for it, but Cody was a master of this type of riding, and he stuck to the bull's tail. The guests got spread out all over the desert. I yelled at the top of my lungs to try and keep them together. But the chase had begun and the horses were taken by it. It was up to the guests now and whatever control over their horses they could muster.

I went into damage-control mode and rode drag, keeping everything in my view. Soon I had no sight of Bully, Cody, or half the riders. At one point I passed a mesquite tree that had a straw hat impaled on its thorns. I expected at any second to come around a corner and find a guest splayed out on the ground.

As I came into the ranch with the last of the riders in front of me I saw Cody and the other riders outside of a pen with Bully in it. I quickly did a head count. Ten. People were laughing, stories were flying. Everybody was safe. But it had all been left up to luck.

I waited until the guests were gone and went to speak to Cody. "What were you doing just taking off like that, man? They weren't ready and everyone got strung out all over the desert."

"Well, we had to get the bull in, that was my priority," he said.

"Your priority? What about the guests?" I asked.

"They made it in okay, didn't they?"

"Yeah, but it was luck. You told me to never leave safety with horses up to luck."

He looked down for a moment and there it was. That look. Tired of it all. "I hear what you're saying," he said. "Makes sense. Come on, let's get these saddles off and go get ourselves a drink."

———————————

It was December and the days were getting colder and darker. One day Alto and I were on a long ride all alone, and I dismounted and sat back against a tree and looked at the horse. I had looked to the horses for answers in the past and now was no different. I thought about what Cody had talked to me about earlier that week.

There's some great ranches up that way, he'd said. *You ever ride that land?*

No. Always wanted to though, I'd replied.

Well, I got connections up there, and my time at Rancho de la Osa, I don't know how much longer I can stay. I could get us jobs up there, on a real horse and cattle ranch, a real outfit. Wyoming, Montana…miles and miles of land that will keep ya feelin' alive.

I looked at Alto. He stared off into the distance, the sound of a bird getting his attention. He seemed to be a happy horse. I had been thinking a lot about that lately. What I had mostly realized was how much I hadn't thought about that in the past. In the beginning horses were horses. They weren't just horses anymore.

I had a strong bond with Alto. *Why?* It started because he was one of the best riding horses on the ranch and that was all I cared about—a good riding horse. What about the other horses? Would they be subjected to a different quality of life just because they weren't as good under saddle? Weren't as fast, weren't as smooth? A horse's quality of life depended solely on how well he did a job for us. It wasn't right.

I looked at Alto. He wasn't mine, I didn't own him. Where would he go when he got old and couldn't carry a human anymore?

Allison. Where was she now?

I would never see the Sunrise, Sunset kids again. Where would they end up?

Karen.

Gus, Scout, Greystone, Smokey…I thought about the Sunset Ranch. A sadness shuddered through me. I did not give back all I should have. All that they deserved. *I didn't know.*

Something swirled around in my heart. I felt a melancholy for all I had seen and done in my time out west. Slowly it turned though. Slowly it turned into something that made sense. All the pieces seemed to come together. Why everything happened. Why I was here. Where I was going. I felt some sort of strength and direction. This was it. All these days had led me here, to this tree, to feel what I was feeling. This was it.

I took a deep breath and looked up into the sky. I felt like I knew that sky. The trees, the rocks, the wind. I felt close to it all. Because I felt close to… myself.

I was quiet on the inside, and it was allowing me to hear my own heart in a way I never had.

That afternoon I asked Cody to talk with me. We stood out in the corrals, the horses about us.

"I wanted to tell you first," I said to him.

"I appreciate that," he said, "and I understand."

"You know, I could live this life forever. I more than half want to go up to those ranches in Wyoming with you."

Cody laughed. "I know, I know. But yer smart, ya see. It's a good life, sure as heck, but I think you have other plans. And if you didn't follow them, it would eat away at ya."

"Yeah," I said solemnly.

"I just hope," Cody started, "that I didn't…ruin your time here at all and that the reason you're leaving isn't partly because of me a bit."

When I saw Cody, I always eventually saw the man as he was with horses—soft, confident, at ease. What I had come to find, though, was that he was like all of us, just trying to find his way.

"Cody, you're the most amazing horseman I have ever known," I said to him. "And what I have learned from you will stay with me for the rest of my life. There will be a part of you in everything I ever do with a horse. I came to this ranch knowing nothing about this job and you gave me a shot, letting me work beside you, teaching me along the way. You didn't have to do that, and I know I wasn't easy to work with sometimes. But you helped me learn more about horses than I could have ever hoped for. I'm lucky to have met you and damn lucky to have you as a friend."

He looked at the ground like he was humbled. "Well, I've learned a lot from you too, Roy. Sometimes the horses and the cowboyin'…sometimes you need other things in yer life too, huh?" Cody looked out over the horses and smiled. "In the end, it's so much closer than ya think."

Later that day I talked to Tom and Monica, and as I expected, they were not too pleased with my decision. I explained to them that my mom was a little down in her health and the fact I was not going to be home for Christmas or any time soon had gotten to her. I felt like I had to make it home. And I wanted to go home. In the end they understood.

When I walked up to Alto it was with a different feeling than I had ever had when I looked at him. For my time on the ranch, he had been my horse, as if I owned him.

How could I say goodbye to him?

Bam-bam-bam!

I shot up in bed. It was five in the morning. Somebody was apparently trying to break my door down. I pulled some pants on and opened it. Lydia stood there, wide-eyed.

"Cody needs you! A horse is hurt!"

I got a shirt and boots on and ran out to the corrals. It was pitch dark. I couldn't see Cody or any of the horses.

"Cody?" I yelled.

"Over here," he answered.

He was at the part of the corrals that had a long cement feed trough that ran along a cement wall. I made my way toward him and slowly my eyes started to make out the situation. I saw Cody's shape, an outline in the dark. He was looking into the feed trough. "Don't get too close!" he warned.

I looked closer and let my eyes adjust to the dark.

A horse had fallen into the trough. The horse was on her back, stuck, legs sticking straight up in the air, hooves shooting out frantically to try and save herself without having any idea how to do it. The horse violently struggled to get out, her breathing simplified down to sharp, sporadic snorts as she twisted and thrusted to get free like a pinned wrestler. But the more my eyes adjusted the more I realized it was all in vain. The cement trough was too deep.

"Who is it?" I asked.

"Can't tell," Cody said as he tried to get near the horse only to be turned away by flailing hooves.

I walked up to where the horse was and tried to calm her while she struggled.

I put my hand on her head. It was warm and sticky. I raised my hand in front of my eyes and rubbed my fingers together. Blood.

"Well come on!" said Cody with a battle cry. He tucked his head and dove in and grabbed a leg and started pulling. I followed. The horse struggled and the legs and hooves suddenly became our enemies as they pulled our arms out of their sockets and kicked at us on all sides. Lydia then came with a spotlight and turned it on so we could see.

It was Rita, mother to a six-month-old foal we had just weaned.

She was completely upside down in the feed trough. In her struggles to get out she had cracked her head against the cement, which was now stained in the dark crimson of horse blood. She lashed out in violent bursts of energy, straining to free herself, smashing her head against the concrete again and again as she fought, until she collapsed in exhaustion.

Cody and I again tried to ease our way in, ducking the flailing hooves. It was no use, we were close to getting seriously hurt ourselves. We had to back off. We stood there in silence, the mare lying there with hardly any life left to her.

Then Cody came up with a plan. "Go get the tractor!" he yelled to me.

The tractor lights didn't work so I drove while shining a flashlight in front of me. When I returned, Cody had two ropes ready. He waited until Rita stopped struggling for a moment, then he dodged in to try to get a loop around a front leg and one around her back leg. It took several rounds of trying but eventually he got it, and we tied the ropes to the back of the tractor.

The mare's breathing slowed and the fight was leaving her. She was giving up. She could have been stuck like this for eight hours for all we knew.

"Go slow and listen to me!" yelled Cody. "I want you to ease forward and stop the moment I say!"

I let up on the clutch and the tractor started to creep ahead. All I needed to use was the clutch and the brake, gently releasing or pressing each. The slack tightened out of the ropes. I felt the weight of the horse as the tractor slowed.

"Keep it going!" yelled Cody.

We moved forward. Rita's thousand-pound body started to be pulled up out of the trough. I had visions of broken legs.

"Slow! Slow!" yelled Cody.

I slowed it down even though it was hardly possible to go much slower.

"Stop! Stop!" he yelled.

He adjusted the ropes.

"Okay, go ahead easy...easy now..."

The horse's body was all contorted. It looked broken in some way.

"Keep it going...keep it going...go...go...stop! We got it!"

Rita's tired body landed beside the trough in a crumpled mass. I quickly put the tractor in reverse to let out some slack as Cody got a halter on her. She was in shock, lying there shaking like she had no idea what happened to her, eyes dazed and blinded by the blood streaking down her head. One of her legs was badly cut and her head was gashed open. We got the ropes off her and Cody urged her to get up. She did. She took a few steps. She looked okay.

Cody walked her around a bit. We got some scissors to cut away some mane and forelock hair to get a better look at the top of her head. There was a pretty big wound.

"I can help her," said Cody.

Cody went to work on the mare, and pretty soon the cut in her head didn't look so bad. It looked as if she was going to be okay.

As we all walked away from each other that morning Cody had a look on his face like he was drained. He didn't talk. The man looked spent.

Later in the day I was walking through the ranch and heard the phone ringing in the office. After twenty rings or so I went to pick it up. It was Monica, who was away in Tucson for the day, and she asked to speak with Cody. I told her I would find him and have him call her back.

I walked to the corrals and the tack room but there was no sign of him.

As I looked around more, I noticed his saddles were gone. Both of them.

And Jake was still in his corral.

I walked up to Cody's cabin. His clothes, his tack, his pictures were all gone.

As I walked past the hacienda and through the courtyard I listened to the steady and predictable jingle of the spurs on every step. I looked at the brim of my Stetson in my silhouette along the buildings as I walked. I walked to Jake and Alto's pen. Jake was enjoying the afternoon in a shaded corner.

I wondered about their goodbye.

Sometimes people go away in your life, but you feel deep down you will see them again, that the part they have to play is not fully done yet. Sometimes you feel it is done though. That two paths that came together for a while have now split.

Cody had left the ranch for good. I thought deep down it was just his way, it was in him, to move on from place to place. There was one thing I knew though, and it was as strong as anything else I had ever known.

He was a good man.

Tom and Monica freaked. They were going into a busy time of year and their head cowboy had left without saying anything. They had a new cowboy coming in two weeks, a guy named Will, who was supposed to replace me. Now they needed a whole lot more than just him. They lined up a couple more guys they knew who could help out. I thought about staying, but my mind was on going home, and my priority had to be getting to Mom's by Christmas. I owed her more than anybody.

For the next couple of weeks, I ran the whole horse program on my own. Morning feeding, the morning trail ride, the care of Rita's wounds, mid-day private riding lessons, the afternoon trail ride and afternoon feeding. Will was due to arrive three days before I left. I would need to spend those three days with him going over everything I could to get him accustomed to the ranch as quickly as possible.

Looming over me was the main thing I had to get done. There were thirty-five or so horses Cody and I had turned out into the Sonora. They needed to be in before the guests started arriving and before Will got here. The problem was I was too busy. I didn't have many guests, but they were all beginners, so I couldn't take them with me to bring in horses. I kept pushing the task back until there was no time left. I had to get it done.

On the morning ride I would take the guests out with the sole focus on searching for horses. If we found some and the riders could handle it, we brought them in. If it was too much for the guests, I would remember where the horses were and after the morning ride was finished, I would ride out again and bring them in. I would then switch my horse out and saddle a fresh one and ride out again to look before the afternoon ride. I rotated between Alto, Jake, and Amarillo. Bit by bit I was getting the loose horses in. Two here, five there. I counted the heads in the corral. More than half were still out. I rode on a couple of far rides, one with Alto and one with Jake, and brought in twelve more. Soon there were just ten stragglers left.

On the guest rides I would look in all the hidden valleys and arroyos near the ranch. In between the guest rides, I would continue to ride out farther and search more difficult terrain. But I just couldn't find those last ten.

Cody had told me about these rolling fields with great grass that were many miles north of the ranch and how now and then horses would make the pilgrimage to that land, to eat and rest and live wild. It was farther out than I had ever ridden.

I waited until I had a free morning. I got up early and fed. I saddled Alto and we rode out of the ranch before sunrise, heading north.

I rode on and on until I was the farthest I had ever been. I was in uncharted territory and unknown land. From Alto's back I looked into the surrounding ironwood and mesquite. The stoic trees stared back with the all-knowing silence of the Sonoran Desert. Hiding nothing, offering nothing.

Something in the dirt caught my eye. I brought Alto to a stop and studied the tracks. The impressions made in the ground were darker than the topsoil. The sun had not yet cooked that upturned dirt.

They were close.

Alto's eyes scanned the hills. He too knew they were close. His chestnut coat and white blaze had turned fuzzy with the cold weather. The tall and lanky, tough desert ranch horse. I softly laid my hand on his neck and his left eye looked back to me and there it was—that feeling I would get with a horse. Something all the way right. A connection to something deep inside me I was fully aware of now.

We rode to the top of a hill and there they were in the valley below. One by one they raised their heads from their peaceful grazing. Alto and I watched the ten horses of different colors in the swaying yellow grass with the righteous mountains behind them. A living painting.

I took off my dusty Stetson and wiped the sweat from my forehead and looked up into the clean blue Arizona sky.

I took a deep breath. The beauty here. The great and powerful silence of a faraway land.

The silence before what was to come.

After standing among the horses and their peace for a bit, we began.

The mesquite trees were now nothing but blurred, jagged shapes as we galloped by them. Alto and I plunged head-first into the cloudy trail of dust that marked the path of the runaway horses. I ducked to one side and then the other as branches narrowly missed taking my head off. Cuts from inch-long mesquite thorns started accumulating...slicing, digging, burning.

We gave chase with raw determination to keep up, to not fall down, to stay in the saddle. Suddenly there was a ditch and without thinking I shifted my weight forward and Alto gathered himself under me and together we left the ground. A silence came over the world.

We hit the ground running, eyes forward. My mind focused on Alto's breathing, a strong and steady puff released into each stride. A machine of nature giving all it had to give. In front of us sprinted four of the horses—the rear of the escaping herd. Dust erupted from under their pounding hooves, suffocating the air, blinding the sight. I would catch glimpses of the others up ahead, but like ghosts, they were only half there in the swirling cloud of dust. Gone, then there, then gone again.

The land opened up and the ten horses poured out onto the grassy flats and now we were running with them in the clear, moving in swift unison, all turning together as if working under one mind. Manes and tails streaming behind like flags and hooves pounding like thundering war drums. The wild horse in them had been reawakened. They were delighted and proud in the graceful movement of their bodies as they stretched over the hard desert land.

What brought me to all of this? I remembered that moment, back in Maine, when I became aware that something had been missing in me my whole life. How I tried hard to move on, but the feeling wouldn't let me go. How it begged me to have the courage to follow it. But I couldn't make sense of it. I was afraid of it.

And then I met horses for the first time.

And now here I was in the Sonoran Desert, communing with horses, dusty and ragged and worn, with a decision in front of me: What to do when I went back.

As I ran after the horses, I realized I wasn't chasing them. I was running with them.

I had been running away too. From an understanding of myself. From the journey within, where you realize that your whole life, is your choice.

We came into the ranch soft and easy and guided the horses into the corral. That was it. They were all in and accounted for.

As we rode up to the hitching post I felt something different in Alto's step. I got down from the saddle and looked at his front left foot. The shoe was half off, the nails tearing through the hoof wall. I got the farrier equipment and gently pried the shoe off. The hoof wall was torn up pretty bad. It looked like it was hurting him.

I looked up at Alto. I didn't know how long the shoe had been like that during the ride. He never let me know in how hard he was working. He never hesitated in anything I asked of him.

I also realized what this meant.

I had taken my last ride with my good friend.

My heart broke for how hard he worked for me, in how he had laid his heart out for me one last time. I let him eat from a flake of hay as I took care of his foot as best I could. As I rubbed him down with a warm cloth I felt what I was trying to get to—a balance of being at one with a horse in the work and in my soul. A balance of caring for each other the best way we could.

I placed my hand on his neck, and he turned his head to me and nuzzled my shoulder, the same way he would my boot when I was riding him.

That afternoon Will arrived. He was from Scotland and in his late twenties. He had been working on a guest ranch in Canada before hearing of the job opening at Rancho de la Osa. We went right to work. I explained everything about the horse operation. I had written out notes on the horses and what each was best at. I wanted him to think of the horses as equal partners and to care for them as best he could and to respect them as individuals. They cared just as much about their lives as we did about ours, and they deserved to be honored for the work they did on this ranch. Will agreed.

"This is Alto," I said.

"Looks like a good horse," Will said.

"I love them all," I said, "but this horse…this horse and I…listen, if you wouldn't mind just looking after him. Making sure he's happy. An extra scratch, an apple now and then. It would mean a great deal to me if you could do that."

"You have my word," he said.

That night Will showed me pictures of the ranch he worked on in Canada and some pictures of Scotland and Europe. He came across a picture of a woman and skipped over it.

"Who is that?" I asked.

He took the picture out. The woman had blonde hair and beautiful eyes. A great smile. He stared at the picture and went quiet for a moment. "That's a woman I used to know," he said, not taking his eyes from the photo. Then he put it back in the stack of pictures and moved on.

I woke up early the next morning. The Grand Prix was once again packed and ready to go. I said my goodbyes. I thanked Tom and Monica for all they had done for me. I wandered through the corral giving each horse a pat, talking for a moment about old times. I would miss my friends. I would give anything to just know they were going to be taken care of.

Jake was lying down in the sun. He was asleep. As I softly walked over to him, I could see his eye lids fluttering and his body twitching. A grunt now and then almost turning into a muffled whinny. He was dreaming.

Horses dream. Just like us. I wondered what he was dreaming of. I wondered what Alto dreamed…if he dreamed about me.

I said goodbye to Jake and told him that he was a great horse and that he would be okay. He could stay relaxed now, that what Cody had taught him he could take with him wherever he went.

I walked over to Alto. He was standing there, content, enjoying the morning sun. I remembered when I first saw him, the gangly and awkward-looking horse. Now all I saw in front of me was a beautiful soul.

I put my hand on his neck and started to cry as I spoke out loud.

"I don't know if I'm gonna be able to say what I'm feeling. You've given me so much, and I ain't talking about the riding and all that. You've given me…you helped me find something inside me that makes me feel…good. Like I'm the person I always wanted to be. There's a place inside myself I can go to and feel like everything is okay. That where I'm at, wherever that is, is alright. That I don't need to be anything else, that I'm not missing anything, that I've got nothing to prove. And all this is with me, it was always with me. And always will be. I just have to let myself feel what's right there.

"I don't feel the hurt like I used to," I said. "And I will forever honor you for how you helped me."

I looked into his eyes.

"I love you, Alto."

I stepped closer and embraced the horse's neck, holding him like that for a long while.

Feeling what was right there.

13 | The Deepest Gladness

HORSES ARE MORE THAN what we think they are. And this is truly discovered the moment we remember *we* are more than we think we are too. The only way we find this out is when we get out of our comfort zone, when we let go of our own lead ropes, take off our halters, and step away from our self-inflicted pressures and let ourselves be free. Many times, it takes unplanned events and breakdowns to get us where we wanted to be all along, breaking from old ways that no longer serve us. Following our hearts and where they lead *is the end in itself*, a beautiful destination that is found in every moment.

This freedom is right there for our taking any time we want it, and once experienced, the most wonderful thing happens:

We wish to give it to all around us.

The horse will not save us. Neither will a journey into the west. Horses and pilgrimages are very much needed and help us in amazing and profound ways. They can surely ignite the spark within us, but in the end, they will only guide us to look back inside ourselves. Horses are here to live their own journeys, and along the way they selflessly help us, again and again. They give so much to us in the strength of their bodies and how they can carry us. They also give so much simply in their presence, in their beauty, and in who and what they are. To see a horse, to know a horse, to touch a horse is the greatest of gifts. It quiets the mind and fills the heart. And it is there, in our hearts, where we will find what we were looking for all along. It is there we will remember it, and it is there we will have it ever after.

And when we feel this, we will revel in that most amazing of opportunities…

To be friends with a horse.

It snowed in New Mexico. Got very cold in Colorado.

The highway feels different when you're going home. There is no rush of adventure. The adventure is over and now you are taking back with you the results—what happened when you put yourself out there.

You may be changed. But was it the change you were looking for?

I drove into Bart's to stay for a night before heading on. In no time I had a beer in one hand and a slice of pizza in the other. He asked about the ranch, but I couldn't go into it much. It was still too heavy on my heart.

"Are you going back to see Karen and the kids?" he asked.

"No," I said. "It won't help her, seeing me again. And the kids, well, I feel I need to just let it be."

We sat and drank for a while.

"What about Allison?" he then asked. "When you get home?"

I contemplated the question. It wasn't like I hadn't thought about it at all on the drive to Bart's. On the whole trip out west. At every ranch, on every horse. About how I would go home, and she would be waiting for me. How when I told her my story, about all the horses, about how I lost half my finger, about Cody and Alto, how she would say it was amazing and how she had missed me and how she wanted to give us another try.

"I love Allison," I said. "She helped me to see things. But that was a different life. It's time to follow this new life."

Bart smiled. Bart knew.

"No regrets, man," he said. "No regrets and being a man with the results."

It was dark when I stopped in Iowa. I thought I was on the outskirts of a town. In the morning I realized it was just the motel and the Grand Prix and blank land stretching out in every direction.

I continued on through Illinois and Indiana and stopped again in Ohio. I stayed the night after that with friends in New York. The next day, Christmas Eve, I drove through New England and into Maine. Snow and cold and a different universe far away from the Sonora. It was dark when I pulled into the driveway. Mom met me at the door and teared up. She looked at my finger and was shocked. I told her it was okay now. She said she could hardly recognize me with the weathered face and long, scraggly beard.

On Christmas there was a major snowstorm. After presents I turned on the television. There was a John Wayne movie marathon. Mom was sitting off to the side, knitting.

"You like John Wayne movies?" she asked.

"Yeah," I said lifelessly without taking my eyes off the TV.

"John Wayne reminds me of your father," she said.

I looked over at her as she sat there with her eyes on her knitting. "Really?" I asked. "He reminds you of Dad?"

She smiled, her eyes still on her knitting.

"In what way?" I asked.

"Well, your father was a police officer and John Wayne was a lawman in most of his movies," she began, continuing to knit like she was talking about nothing special. "Or at least he was usually playing a respected man who was out to do the right thing. Everybody in town knew your father and they respected him. They would go to him with their problems and such. He would always look out for people. He would always tell it like it was and if he had something to say, he'd say it." She paused before going on. "They also had the same manner. Your father was a tall man, and he had a swagger to his walk, and a certain swagger to his voice that was charismatic and commanding at the same time."

"Did Dad like John Wayne movies?" I asked.

"Loved them."

"Really?"

"Oh yes. You don't remember? He used to always put them on, usually Sunday afternoons, and you used to sit in his lap watching them with him."

I stared at the carpeted floor as if by doing so long enough, hard enough, it would help me remember.

"Do you know which ones were his favorites?" I eagerly asked.

"No, but if one was on he'd watch it. My favorite is the one where John is in Ireland and—"

"*The Quiet Man,* yeah," I interrupted. I was smiling.

"Yes, *The Quiet Man,* that's a great one."

I turned my chair away from the TV so I could face my mom as we talked. As she sat there knitting and telling stories about my father, I realized how much of a good person she was. Not just as my mother, but as a person.

Horses had taught me to see the insides.

Spring came around. There was a small park in Portland with nice fence posts. People walking or driving by would stop to watch, wondering what I was doing.

The feel of the lariat in my hands building the loop. The sound of it twirling over my head. Watching the loop sail through the air, and then the zip of the rope as it tightened around the post. It felt good. There were no cattle to rope so a metal fence post in a city park had to do.

I was living back in Portland and working as a bartender again.

The apartment market was tight. I had called up my old landlord to see if he had anything open, and he had one place right in the middle of town. I took it. It looked like my old apartment. I got a job at a restaurant that was opening up. Just like when I first came to Portland a long time ago.

I was back to my old life.

As usual I searched to find what horse barns were near me. I made calls and talked with some people, but nothing felt right. The horse culture in Maine was very different than what I had experienced in the West, and I just didn't see where I would fit.

The Grand Prix had broken down two days after I returned home. The mechanic said I was lucky, that it could have quit on me any time in the past year. He told me it needed a lot of work that would cost four times what the car was worth. I asked him what it was worth, and he said two hundred dollars.

"We would really just be taking it off your hands," he said. "It will just go up north and be picked for parts."

That car had gotten me everywhere I needed to be at for over eight years. It was my partner through it all, the good and bad.

Just before the deal with the mechanic was finalized, I went back to the Grand Prix and pulled off the radio dial and put it in my pocket.

I was at work a few weeks later when Allison's friend Natalie came in for dinner.

"I heard about you," she started, "that you were on some ranch somewhere in Texas or something, doing something with horses. How did that happen?" She said like it was all very strange.

I didn't know how to answer. "Well, I was very fortunate to…be able to go to some different places and…meet some horses."

My response didn't seem to make sense to her. She seemed to have something else she was getting ready to say though.

"Oh, well it must have been awesome. Did you hear Allison is married?"

"No. I didn't."

"She got married just a few months ago."

Natalie waited for my response. I thought about it. Allison, married. What did that mean to me?

"Is she happy?" I asked.

"Ahh, yes," said Natalie, as if not expecting the question. "Yeah, she's really happy."

I smiled. A real smile, uncontainable. I was very happy at that moment for Allison. A great woman. I was happy she was happy.

"Good," I said.

I was a good bartender but there was something hanging over me and people could feel it. The change was too drastic. From running with horses over the hot Sonoran Desert to getting dressed up and serving drinks in cold Maine. I worked five days a week and hung out with old friends on the weekends. People wanted to hear stories about the ranches, and I tried to tell them, but I wasn't into it. Eventually, when out, I would wind up sitting by myself in the corner, thinking about Alto, Scout, Drumbeat, and the others.

Ben was a farmer. He worked nights at the restaurant while writing a proposal to start up a community-supported organic farm. He seemed to live life right. He was a person who knew his passion and was dynamically pursuing it.

"So you're working at getting your own farm," I ventured one night while we were talking.

"It's my dream," Ben said smiling. "My soul's calling."

"That's awesome. I have all the respect for that, having a dream and going for it with all you got."

"Yeah, like with what you've done and what you're doing."

I chuckled. "What, bartending?"

"No, your work with horses."

"Yeah, it was an amazing time out west, but it's weird how it all ended up. Back at the beginning."

Ben smiled like he knew something I didn't. "You're at the beginning. Just not the beginning, I think, that you think it is."

I considered that. "Out west there were these ranches and these people who all gave me a chance. Here in Maine, I've looked and searched and talked to people and nothing feels... right."

"Well maybe there's a reason it doesn't feel right. Maybe working at another ranch isn't *supposed* to feel right. The universe wants us to find our way and if we put in the heart and hard work sooner or later the universe steps up. But when you get close to the thing, the *real* thing, there is a...a leap of faith, and you have to take it on your own. You don't get it from anybody else. Not from a barn, a barn owner...not even a horse."

I stared down at the copper surface of the bar.

"Maybe it's not about a horse ranch that will take you in anymore," continued Ben, "or a barn owner that will hire you or even a horse that you will meet. Maybe it's about you now, and what you're going to choose to do on your own. That's the *real* beginning."

That night I lay in bed with my eyes wide open, staring at the ceiling, just as I had in Colorado, in California, in Arizona. I thought about the two horses I met the night Allison and I broke up. I didn't even know their names. But they felt like old friends I had been through a lot with. I had seen something in their eyes, and it sent me on a journey to find some sort of understanding somewhere out there. Something that would save me.

I closed my eyes and there they were again in my head, those two horses, staring at me. This time, though, the look was different. They didn't have the answers. They weren't putting any ideas in my head. They weren't trying to save me.

They were waiting to see what I was going to do.

I got up and walked to the computer and turned it on and sat down. I went on the internet to a local horse-related message board and started typing:

I will travel to work with horses of all ages and levels of training, from starting work to finishing work. My philosophy is I like the horse to be a friend and willing partner to a person who uses safe and gentle ways based on clear communication. My number-one priority is to help establish a bond between horse and human based on patience, consistency, respect, understanding, and most important of all, trust. Please feel free to contact me to further discuss my methods and philosophies.

I was nervous driving to my first client. The woman's name was Ella, and she had a six-year-old Quarter Horse mare named Paloma. Paloma was very spirited and only had a little bit of previous training. Ella wanted to work with her and hopefully ride her, but the horse's energy was intimidating. I worked with Paloma first and then Ella worked with her. By the end of the first session, we were quietly riding Paloma around the ring and Ella asked if I could come out weekly.

My next clients had Tennessee Walkers they needed help with. The client after that had an Appaloosa we rode for the first time. These people told their friends. Soon I had more calls.

Soon I had a waiting list.

Within a year I was being asked to present horsemanship clinics.

Each time it worked just like it had so many times before. When I got around horses everything just clicked into place. Everything was right, inside and out. I found helping people to find this within themselves and to connect in their own way to their horses was just as fulfilling as anything I did with the horses myself. It was what all people wanted—*to connect with their horses in their own unique way*. They were just like me, searching for something within, and finding it through horses.

Writer and theologian Frederick Buechner once said, *Our calling is where our deepest gladness and the world's hunger meet*. There is a path unique to each of us. When we find it and feel how it fills us, we are inspired to help others experience the very same thing.

One day I was driving back from working with a horse. I watched as the land passed by. A house, a field, a farm, a stone wall, a patch of trees. I was smiling. It was all so beautiful. Everything. It couldn't *not* be beautiful. It all started to churn up inside of me, a swirling energy. It built up until I couldn't ignore it, it had to be released. I turned off the radio. I pulled the car over. The air was crisp as I got out and walked into the field. I stood in the grass and the wind blew around me and I thought about the yellow grass of the Sonora. The brambly grass of the Hollywood Hills. The swaying grass talking to me from either side of western highways.

It was all so beautiful. Everything was beautiful. Life was beautiful.

I dropped down to my knees and put my hands to the ground.

I looked up into the sky.

"Thank you," I said.

The people who had the Tennessee Walkers said they were rescuing a new foal and they asked me to help with him. He was five months old and had never been touched before. He was very wild. I drove to their barn to meet the little guy. He had been there a few days, and I was told he was very scared and defensive and nobody was able to get near him.

I walked into the barn and there was a group of people looking at the little colt as he stood in his stall. He was not tall enough to look out through the bars yet. I peered in at him. When I opened the door, he ran to the back corner of the stall and hid his face, positioning his hind end to defend against anything bad. He was a palomino with a white blaze and four white socks, his little tail pinned to his butt. Legs dancing in fear. If he could have climbed the wall, he would have.

"What's his name?" I asked.

"Rocky," someone replied.

Rocky. He was so scared. Not knowing where he was, not knowing what to do. Not feeling good on the inside.

I knew what that felt like.

I thought about Oberon, Kassari, Prairie Drumbeat, Major Headline, Nocturne, Greystone, Scout, Gus, Smokey, Jake. Alto. They had helped me, and I never felt like I was able to repay them in the way they deserved.

But this horse was here. Rocky was here with me now.

Gone was the thought of what horses could do for me.

"Rocky…" I said quietly to myself.

I walked into the stall and closed the door behind me. I leaned up against it, let out a deep breath, and waited. After a while, I don't know how long, his movement quieted. An ear came forward in my direction. His head turned to me.

"What are you going to do?" someone asked.

Rocky looked at me. His eyes were opening up, letting their guard down, wondering who I was, what may be.

When you look into a horse's eyes you see the soul of a beautiful being. What it also helps you to do is see inside yourself.

I smiled the simplest most perfect smile I have ever felt.

"We've already begun," I said softly.

Rocky.

He didn't know what all this was yet.

I did though. They had taught me that.

And now I was ready to give back.

Acknowledgments

FIRST AND FOREMOST, my sincere gratitude to you, the reader, for signing on for this story and for making it here with me now as I share my gratitude. From my heart—thank you for coming along with me.

The events in these pages took place between the years of late 2000 and early 2003. During that time never did I think, *Hey, maybe this would make a good book*. It wasn't until I returned home to Maine that I thought to write down what happened and where it happened and how it happened. That turned into a writing project that lasted about ten years, culminating in a book I self-published in 2013. It was well-supported by the horse community in Maine, and I loved that journey very much, but I always thought the story could reach out a little farther than it did. And for this I now have Trafalgar Square Books to thank. Rebecca, Martha, Caroline, and everyone at Trafalgar Square Books are an exceptional team that I am eternally grateful for.

I am also so very thankful for my friends. From the earliest ones to the new ones to those yet to meet, both two-legged and four-legged, my heart lives in constant gratitude for the friendship, love, and support I feel. One of these friends is Joe Camp. It was when he appeared in my life with his kind but "now is not the time to be polite" honesty that *Land of the Horses* really came together. Joe has helped literally millions of dogs, horses, and humans in his life, and now he can add one more to the list.

Over the last twenty years I have experienced so much support, patience, and trust from so many people and their horses. When people have me out to their homes or to work with them at a clinic, all with the belief I have something to offer, that honor is never lost on me. The opportunity to work with people and their horses is a gift of the highest order. It's a great "coming together" where we all learn from each other, and where I can learn how to be of better service to the world.

I believe when someone takes a picture that what is being felt inside the photographer can be just as important as what is in the image. There's a glow in Kim Graham's eye when she is behind a camera, and the photo on the cover of this book is courtesy of her. I am so thankful for what she captured.

My mother and father, Pat and David Lombard, are pillars of love. Through them I learned how to best support those I love. Learning by example is one of the greatest ways you can be given anything, and from them I have learned a lot.

To Alto and all the other horses from this story who had patience with me, knowing my heart and where it was coming from even while my ways were young, rushed, and insecure—you have my biggest thanks.

Matea walks beside me through all of life. In her one blue eye and one brown I see all the love there is. Thank you for this, Tay Dog. Thank you for your beautiful dog heart.

And to Rocky the palomino horse: Our road together is eighteen years strong. We have known each other in our beginnings, we have been there through each other's challenges, and we have felt the depth of each other's hearts. In learning how to best listen to him I have learned how to best listen to myself. I feel so lucky to have him in my life. So honored by our journey together. So thankful for the connection we share.

So thankful to be friends with Rocky.

About the Author

CHRIS LOMBARD works with people and their horses to help them connect with each other. He travels all over the United States, working with people both privately and in clinics. There is challenge, joy, and much opportunity for growth when learning alongside a horse, and Chris's focus is to help people get a feel for their own individual path in that journey.

In recent years Chris and his horse, Rocky, have been featured at many expos, fairs, and horse shows. He is also the author of *The Horses in Our Stars: A Story of Life, Love, and the Journey Within,* an account of how connecting with horses can help us to understand the love and fear in our lives. This has led Chris to speak at many different schools, libraries, and special events. He also writes essays on nature and horsemanship that have appeared in many different magazines.

Chris currently lives in Maine and continues to be inspired by horses, what they show us, and the journey we take with them. You can learn more about him at www.ChrisLombard.com.